—— 1907-11 ——

MANCHESTER UNITED

The First Halcyon Years

Mark Metcalf

Foreword by
Martin Buchan

AMBERLEY

ACKNOWLEDGEMENTS

The author would like to thank the following people for their help with this book: Martin Buchan, Jim Fox, Robert Boyling, George Orr, Roger Booth, David Wood, Paul Days, Ruth Jones, Peter Holme, Tom Furby, Emily Tinker and the library staff at Manchester, Bolton, Sheffield and Sunderland.

First published 2014

Amberley Publishing
The Hill, Stroud, Gloucestershire, GL5 4EP
www.amberley-books.com

Copyright © Mark Metcalf, 2014

The right of Mark Metcalf to be identified as the Author of this work has been asserted in accordance with the Copyrights, Designs and Patents Act 1988.

ISBN 978 1 4456 2238 5 (print)
ISBN 978 1 4456 2261 3 (ebook)

British Library Cataloguing in Publication Data.
A catalogue record for this book is available from the British Library.

Typesetting by Amberley Publishing.
Printed in Great Britain.

CONTENTS

FOREWORD

I am delighted to have been asked to write the foreword for this book, which documents United's first FA Cup success and Charity Shield exploits, as I had the honour of captaining the team in the drawn Charity Shield fixture against Liverpool, the First Division Champions, at Wembley in 1977. We qualified to take part in that match by beating our Anfield rivals in that year's FA Cup final, when we denied them a famous Treble, as they went on to win the European Cup in Rome the following week.

Sadly, unlike the stars of 1907–11, I have no League titles to celebrate, but feel privileged to have served the club for eleven and a half seasons. Part of my current role at the Professional Footballers' Association is informing members of the PFA's history and how the founding members of the union, led by Billy Meredith, were locked out of their place of work for daring to become affiliated to the National Federation of Trade Unions. In my previous job as Football Promotions Manager with sports company Puma, I was able, through my friendship with Sir Alex, to sign up the young Ryan Giggs to wear our boots for a couple of seasons.

In our video presentation to members, a photograph of Billy, one of United's first 'superstars', morphs into Ryan standing in a similar pose. For me, it is a fitting reminder of the part played in those early days of the club by a group of players who are now, by way of this book, receiving the recognition they deserve.

Martin Buchan

INTRODUCTION

Manchester United Football Club was formed in 1878 as Newton Heath (Lancashire & Yorkshire Railway) Football Club. It entered the Football League in 1892, but by the start of the 1907/08 season, had won neither the Division One title nor the FA Cup.

The club changed its name in April 1902, and won promotion to Division One at the end of the 1905/06 season, finishing runners-up to champions Bristol City. At first, the club played home games at North Road, Newton Heath, but by 1907, Bank Street in Clayton was the club's home (although discussions about a move to the other side of the city were already underway).

Between September 1907 and April 1908, Manchester United thrilled their growing band of supporters and provided the platform for the club's long-term success by racing to the Division One title for the first time in the club's history. They achieved this by creating what was then a League record fifty-two points (there were two points for a win, one for a draw) in a League of twenty teams. Success was achieved on the back of a ten-game winning streak between September and November 1907, which included beating the then League champions Newcastle United 6-1 away.

At the start of the following season, they became the first winners of the FA Charity Shield by beating QPR (winners of the Southern League) 4-0.

Ernest Mangnall, the club's first great manager, managed the Manchester United side. The following season he plotted a first-ever FA Cup success when, after beating Brighton, Everton, Blackburn

Rovers, Burnley and Newcastle United, they beat Bristol City 1-0 in the Cup final, played at the Crystal Palace. Sandy Turnbull scored the only goal, and yet at the start of the following season he was prepared to join with his teammates, as well as players from other clubs, in refusing to play unless the hated maximum wage for footballers was abolished. Their struggle was to end in defeat.

Later, in February 1910, Manchester United moved across the city to play their opening match at a magnificent new stadium, Old Trafford. Although they lost 4-3 to Liverpool, the remaining seven League home games of the season were to be won, with Manchester United establishing their new home as a fortress from the very start.

That was certainly the case the following season, when just one match was lost and four drawn in nineteen home League fixtures. The result was a second League success as well as a second Charity Shield when Manchester United walloped Southern League champions Swindon Town 8-4.

Two League titles, an FA Cup success and two Charity Shield triumphs meant that the 1907–11 period was the start of Manchester United's long road to becoming the most successful English club ever. But who were the players and management team that set the Manchester club on the road to greatness? Who were their opponents? What sort of football was played and who watched it? Find out more inside.

1

Building a Great Side

Manchester United finished the 1906/07 season in eighth place in Division One, with forty-two points from thirty-eight games; this was nine points behind champions Newcastle United.

Confidence must have been high among the players, however, as statistics show that following the team's reshuffle, starting at home to Aston Villa on New Year's Day 1907, Manchester United improved immensely to capture twenty-four points from seventeen matches to rise up the table from fifteenth place. During the same period, Newcastle had played eighteen games and taken twenty-three points.

The key to the improvements in the club's fortunes had, ironically, come at Hyde Road, home of rivals Manchester City. Having been relegated from the First Division at the end of the 1901/02 season, City, under the direction of manager Tom Maley, forged their way back up the following season.

Then in 1903/04, City captured the FA Cup by beating Bolton in the final, and might even have done 'the double' of League and Cup, but they finished second to 'the Wednesday' in the race for the League title. Such rapid improvement had not gone unnoticed. But when the Football Association (FA) undertook an enquiry into City's rapid upturn in fortunes, they found only some minor irregularities. Things came to a head at the end of the following season, when only a last-day defeat at Aston Villa denied City the title. Afterwards, Alec Leake, the Villa captain, complained that City's outside-right, Billy Meredith, had offered him £10 to throw the game.

After an inquiry, Meredith was found guilty by the FA; he was among several players fined a total of £900 and suspended from playing football for a year. Manchester City refused to provide financial help for him, and so he decided to go public about what really was going on at the club, making the following comment to newspapers:

> What was the secret of the success of the Manchester City team? In my opinion, the fact that the club put aside the rule that no player should receive more than four pounds a week ... The team delivered the goods, the club paid for the goods delivered and both sides were satisfied.

Such a statement indicated that Manchester City had broken the maximum wage rule. This was bound to alert the FA, who once again was forced to carry out another investigation into the financial activities of Manchester City. Maley was interviewed and he admitted that he had followed what seemed like standard English practice by making additional payments to all the players. He claimed that if all First Division clubs were investigated 'not four would come out unscathed'.

As a result of their investigation, the FA suspended Tom Maley from football for life. Seventeen players were fined and suspended until January 1907, after which, with the FA ruling that they could not play for City again, they were to be sold. In protest, Billy Gillespie, centre-forward in the 1904 FA Cup final, refused to pay his fine and instead emigrated to the United States, where he died in 1942.

Manchester City put the offending players up for sale at an auction at the Queen's Hotel in Manchester, which appears to have been rigged in advance; four of the best were snapped up by the bowler-hatted Mangnall, with City getting nothing for Meredith, who had scored 145 goals in 338 games. This was something of a bargain to put it mildly.

Mangnall's other purchases were Herbert Burgess, Alex 'Sandy' Turnbull and Jimmy Bannister. The latter was to prove a reliable partner for Meredith on United's right wing for a number of seasons, while Sandy scored many goals from Meredith's crosses. Sandy and Meredith were to enjoy almost thirteen years of playing together.

Mangnall had outwitted his rivals by arranging the deals with Manchester City in advance. United already had a relationship with Meredith by dint of the fact that the money he had obtained to set up his sports equipment shop in St Peter's Square in the city centre had come from John Henry Davies, the Manchester United chairman. Whether that helped, no one can be absolutely certain. It is arguable that no Manchester United manager ever did better business than when Ernest Mangnall signed four Manchester City players at the end of 1906, all of who made their debuts on New Year's Day 1907.

Mangnall had been appointed to the post of United manager, or secretary as the post was then called, on 30 September 1903. He replaced Jim West on the recommendation of Manchester United director and Football League president J. J. Bentley.

Rescued from Bankruptcy

Less than eighteen months earlier, the club had been on the brink of going out of business, with debts of £2,670, only to be saved at the last minute when five local businessmen, including brewery owner John Henry Davies, came forward to take over the club's debts. The entrepreneurs had been persuaded by club captain and pub owner Harry Stafford, who also put up £200 of his own money, to take control of the club. Those involved must have been well aware that a successful football club would reflect well on themselves and possibly increase future business opportunities.

It was Davies, a self-made man, who provided Mangnall with £3,000 to seek out players good enough to take Manchester United back into Division One, a task made even more urgent by Manchester City's promotion in 1902/03.

Bolton-born Mangnall was able, in his first year, to bring in what proved to be three mainstays of the 1907/08 title-winning side: 'keeper Harry Moger, Charlie Roberts and Dick Duckworth. However, gaining promotion did not come easily and Manchester United twice finished third in 1903/04 and 1904/05, before achieving promotion in 1905/06.

Having initially struggled, the side's fine form in the second half of the 1906/07 season meant that Ernest Mangnall's dealings in the transfer market during the close season were mainly designed to boost his reserve forces. United did sign James Turnbull from Southern League side Leyton in May for what was described as a 'heavy fee' in the papers. Bob Bonthron, after 134 first team appearances, was moved on to Sunderland after losing his regular place in the side to Dick Holden towards the end of the previous campaign.

Ernest Mangnall's 1907 Summer Transfer Dealings
In:

Herbert Broomfield [G], Bolton Wanderers
George Stacey [FB], Barnsley
Jimmy [James] Turnbull [F], Leyton FC
Kerr Whiteside [HB], Irvine Victoria
Tom Wilcox [G], Blackpool

Also arriving were several players who were either signed from the clubs listed or signed after they had been released and were free agents. None ever made a first team match.

P. McLarney, Norwich City
Mills, Willenhall Pickwick, Walsall
Handcock [F], Hyde
Routledge [F], Hooley Hill.

Out – including total appearances and goals scored for Manchester United:

Tommy Blackstock [FB], died [34/0]
Bob Bonthron [FB], Sunderland [134/3]
Frank Buckley* [HB], Aston Villa [3/0]
Vince Hayes [FB], Brentford – later returned [128/2]
Alexander 'Sandy' Robertson [F], Bradford [34/10]
Charlie Sagar [F], Atherton FC [33/24]
Alexander Robertson, unknown [35/1]
Bob Valentine [G], Swinton RLFC [10/0]
Tommy Arkesden, Gainsborough Trinity [79/33]
Clem Beddow [F], Burnley [34/15]
Joe Williams [F], unknown [3/1]
Alf Schofield [F], retired [179/35]

*Franklin Charles Buckley is better known as Major Frank Buckley following his First World War exploits. He later became a famous manager with spells in charge at Norwich, Blackpool, Wolverhampton Wanderers, Notts County, Hull City, Leeds United and Walsall.

2

THE BUILD-UP TO
THE 1907/08 SEASON

There was an unusual start to the season for some of the United players when they lined up twice against Bolton Wanderers over the first weekend in August to play the American game of pushball. Never before seen in Britain, this attracted a large crowd on the Saturday at the Royal Lancashire Show just outside Bolton to see both teams attempt to push a ball weighing 56 pounds (4 stone) into each other's goal. There was laughter when the ball rolled over the players, with both matches finishing in a draw at 1-1 and 2-2. The papers predicted the game was unlikely to catch on in Britain!

In the event, the United players must have heaved a sigh of relief when the first Reds *v.* Whites practice match on a bright sunny day took place on Saturday 17 August.

Reds: Moger, Holden, Burgess, Duckworth, Roberts, Bell, Berry, Picken, Menzies, Mills, Williams [H].

Whites: Broomfield, McLarney, Stacey, Downie, Thomson, McGillivray, Meredith, Bannister, J. Turnbull, Dyer, Wall.

The good gate meant a number of charities would benefit. Those who had made the effort to get to Bank Street got the chance to see James Turnbull in a United shirt for the first time, but also goalkeeper Herbert Broomfield, who had signed at the very end of the previous season from Bolton Wanderers. Another debutant was George Stacey, signed for £200 from Barnsley to understudy

Herbert Burgess at left-back, but who was to go on to have a fine first season at United?

The Whites won the first practice match 4-3, James Dyer opening the scoring and Wall scoring the second before Menzies and Williams levelled at half-time.

Playing for the Reds, Alex Menzies was the man most likely to make way for James Turnbull in the first team after being singled out as the weak link in the United five man forward line in the previous season's match reports.

Manchester United was to start the season with an away day fixture against Aston Villa. The side had lost 2-0 at Villa Park in the final away fixture of 1906. As this was prior to the signing of the Manchester City players, the result at the start of the new season would provide a good indicator of how the side might fare in the coming season. Aston Villa had last won the First Division title in 1900; this, their fifth success, made them the most successful side ever at this time.

Pen Profiles of the Manchester United First Team in the 1907/08 Season

Goalkeepers

Harry Moger moved to United in May 1903 from Southampton, FA Cup finalists in 1900 and 1902, after finding his opportunities restricted by England international Jack Robinson. Although it took him until the start of the 1904/05 season to become a regular between the United posts, his ever-increasing confidence over the intervening years meant he began the 1907/08 season assured of his place in the side. He was to make 264 League and FA Cup appearances for Manchester United, and his fine performances helped the club win two League titles, two Charity Shields and the FA Cup. It was surprising that the 'keeper never played for England. Moger was a big man, standing at 6 feet 2 inches.

Herbert Broomfield signed from Bolton at the end of the previous season. With Moger in fine form, he was to find his first team opportunities restricted, and he was forced to wait until March 1908 before making his first team debut. He was associated with the Players' Union from its start, and was appointed secretary of the organisation in 1908.

Full-Backs

Dick Holden had signed for United in May 1904 and made his debut against Blackpool the following April. When regular full-back Bob Bonthron had been injured the following season, Holden took the chance to make the position his own. The 1907/08 season was to be his finest at the club as he missed out on an FA Cup final place in 1909 and also missed out, due to an injury, on a second League championship winners' medal in 1910/11.

Herbert Burgess was one of four Manchester City players signed by Ernest Mangnall in December 1906, after City had won the FA Cup in 1904 when Billy Meredith's single goal overcame Bolton Wanderers in the final. Although Burgess was only 5 foot 5 inches tall, he more than made up for his lack of height with his pace and surprising upper body strength. At the start of the 1907/08 season, Burgess had played four times for England. A badly damaged knee forced him to retire in 1910 at age twenty-six.

George Stacey signed from Barnsley in the summer of 1907 at a reported fee of £200. He was to go on and have a long spell at Manchester United, making 267 first team appearances in a career shortened by the First World War. Nicknamed 'Silent' because he was a man of few words, Stacey did his talking on the pitch.

Ted Dalton played his only game for United at Anfield in March 1908, when, in a remarkable game, Liverpool won 7-4.

Aaron Hulme signed from Oldham Athletic in May 1906. The Manchester-born fullback was to make only one appearance against Preston North End on the final day of the League season. He moved to Nelson at the end of the following season after playing just three more first team games.

Half-Backs

Richard 'Dick' Duckworth: Manchester born and bred, Duckworth became a half-back after agreeing to swap from his centre-forward position for a reserve-team derby match with Manchester City on Christmas Day 1903. However, it wasn't until he forced his way past Alex Downie during the 1906/07 season that Duckworth became a regular in the United side. Once established, he went on to play some marvellous matches and helped form a formidable half-back line-up with Roberts and Bell. Duckworth was one of United's greatest pre-First World War players and the winner of two

League titles and the FA Cup. He made 251 first team appearances for Manchester United.

Charlie Roberts: Darlington's most famous footballer cost United a reported fee of £600, a huge sum at the time, to sign him from Grimsby at the end of the 1903/04 season. It was to prove money well spent; Roberts went on to play some magnificent games at centre-half, where his tackling, passing and pace, in addition to his captaining skills, made him into one of the club's all-time greats. The fact that he was only capped three times by England has much to do with Roberts being one of staunchest supporters of the fledgling Players' Union and its chairman until September 1921. Oldham Athletic paid a club record fee of £1,750 to sign him in August 1913, and in 1914/15 he captained the Latics to their highest-ever position of second in the First Division championship.

Alex Bell: Born in South Africa to Scottish parents, Bell cost United £700 when he was signed, originally as a centre-forward, from Ayr Parkhouse in January 1903. Pushed into action at half-back he soon turned the left-half position into his own from where he was quietly effective. After winning two League titles with United and an FA Cup winners' medal, he later won the League title with Blackburn Rovers in the 1913/14 season. Bell was awarded just a single cap for Scotland.

Ernest Thomson: Signed from Darwen in May 1906, Thomson was to find his first-team path blocked by the Duckworth, Roberts and Bell half-back line-up that provided United's backbone. He made his debut at Middlesbrough in September 1907, but by the time he moved on to Nelson in 1909, Thomson had made only three further first team appearances.

John McGillivray was unfortunate to be cast in the role of understudy to Charlie Roberts. McGillivray's first-team debut was against Blackpool in the FA Cup in January 1908, and he made his first of just three United League appearances the following weekend in a 2-0 defeat at Sheffield United. He moved to Southport Central in 1910.

Kerr Whiteside made his only United appearance at Sheffield United in January 1908 and was to leave the club three years later to join Hurst, where he enjoyed a long association.

Alex Downie: By now in his thirties, Downie had joined Manchester United from Swindon Town in October 1902 and had been a regular in the side until 1906/07, when Duckworth replaced him at right-half. He was to enjoy a well-earned benefit match in February 1908. By the time he left the club in the summer of 1909, he was only nine matches short of 200 United first team appearances.

Forwards

Billy Meredith was one of the all-time greatest footballers, who would have been a star in whatever era he played. Manchester City signed the former miner from Northwich Victoria in 1894, beginning a thirty-year association with Manchester that delighted supporters.

Having helped City to the Second Division title, the Welshman was part of the side that beat Bolton Wanderers in the 1904 FA Cup final, in which he scored the only goal of the game. His first spell with Manchester City was to come to an end in December 1906, when he and three other players transferred across the city to United. After collecting two Division One League winner's medals, along with another FA Cup winner's medal, Meredith moved back to play for City in 1921, and even appeared in an FA Cup semi-final three years later in his fiftieth year.

Meredith, who had a habit of chewing a toothpick as he made his way down the wings, won an incredible forty-eight caps for his country during a period when matches with the other home nations were the staple fare.

James Bannister: After winning a Second Division championship medal in 1903 with Manchester City, the Leyland-born forward missed out on an FA Cup final appearance the following season. One of four players signed from City in December 1906, Bannister made his debut at home to Aston Villa on New Year's Day 1907. During the 1907/08 season he missed only two games. He joined Preston North End in October 1909.

Alex Menzies had won the Scottish Cup with Hearts in 1906 before moving south in November of the same year. Although he scored on his League debut, he struggled to make an impact in front of goal. His days were numbered when United signed James Turnbull, and he moved on swiftly, signing for Luton Town in September 1907.

George Wall: Very fast, tricky and with a wonderful knack of cutting inside and surprising 'keepers with his shooting, the outside-left was a match for any full-back. During the 1907/08 season he performed with distinction. The Sunderland-born man was to have a fine career at Manchester United, winning two League and one FA Cup winners' medals and making 316 first-team appearances, during which he notched ninety-eight goals. Wall had made his international debut playing against Wales in March 1907, and was to go on and play five times for his country.

Alexander 'Sandy' Turnbull was another player signed in 1906 from Manchester City, where he won the Second Division championship in 1903 and the FA Cup in 1904. Brilliant in the air, he was on the end of many of Meredith's accurate crosses and corners. Turnbull was to finish as United's top scorer in the 1907/08 season, and later scored the Cup final winning goal in the 1909 final against Bristol City. Turnbull also scored the first goal at Old Trafford in February 1910. Heavily involved in a match-betting scandal in 1915, Turnbull later joined the Footballers' Battalion and was killed on active service in France on 3 May 1917.

James Turnbull arrived at Bank Street in the summer of 1907, after scoring fifteen goals for Leyton in the Southern League the previous season. After replacing Alex Menzies at centre-forward, he went on to forge a lethal partnership with his namesake 'Sandy' Turnbull during the 1907/08 and 1908/09 seasons. When he returned home to Scotland in 1910, United were to sign 'Knocker' West from Nottingham Forest as his replacement.

William Berry: Sunderland-born, he joined Manchester United in November 1906 from Southern League side Tottenham Hotspur while the club was awaiting the arrival of Billy Meredith, signed in May 1906 but unavailable until 1 January 1907. Berry made nine appearances during the 1906/07 season, but was to play only three times during the 1907/08 season. He joined Stockport County in February 1909.

Jack Picken: The Scotsman had scored on his League debut at home to Bristol City in September 1905, a season in which he was to finish as the club's leading scorer with thirty goals when United won promotion to Division One. Having found goals much more difficult to come by in Division One, Picken was to enjoy few opportunities during the 1907/08 season, but he was to later play enough games during the 1910/11 season to qualify for a League championship medal during a season when United captured the title for a second time.

Tommy Wilson: The well-travelled Preston-born forward made his only Manchester United appearance against Blackburn Rovers at home in February 1908. He was to manage Rochdale after the war.

Harold Halse signed for Manchester United in March 1908, with Southend United, for whom he had scored 200 goals, receiving £350 for his services. He made a goal-scoring debut against The Wednesday. He later gained an FA Cup winners' medal with United in 1909, and did the same with Aston Villa in 1913 before also playing in the FA Cup final for Chelsea in 1915, the Londoners losing out in the final to Sheffield United 3-0 at Old Trafford.

Harry Williams made only one appearance in 1907/08. Signed from Burnley in July 1903, he played thirty-six times in the Manchester United first team, scoring eight goals.

In October 1907, Ernest Mangnall signed David Christie from Hurlford FC and Joe Ford from Crewe Alexandra in October 1907. Both were forwards who went on to make two and five first team appearances for Manchester United respectively. Then in February 1908, Ernest Mangnall signed Joe Curry, a half-back from Scotswood FC, and Tommy Wilson, a forward from Leeds City. Curry was to make fourteen first team appearances in his career at Manchester United, and Wilson played just the once.

The Secretary/Manager

James Ernest Mangnall was a surprise choice when he was appointed as Manchester United's secretary/manager in the autumn of 1903. He had been the club secretary at Bolton in their 1898/99 relegation season, and later secretary/manager at Burnley when the Turf Moor side was relegated the following season. Mangnall's integrity had also been questioned when the Burnley 'keeper Jack Hillman had been found guilty of trying to bribe Nottingham Forest players to lose the last game of the season to help his side avoid relegation, for which the 'keeper was banned for a year.

Mangnall was known to preach a gospel of physical fitness and team spirit and, typical of most English League managers up until the 1970s, believed that players should see relatively little of the ball during the week, and especially at the start of it, in order to ensure that they were hungry for it on Saturdays. As he had no previous reputation for getting his sides to play good football, there was little to suggest he would prove a success at Manchester United. But a success he was, going on to take the side back up into Division One, where he oversaw two League title triumphs, an FA Cup success and two Charity Shield triumphs before he decided to move to Manchester City.

Football in 1907

Football in 1907 was very different to today. Firstly, there were no substitutes, so if a player got injured he was usually required to limp out the match on the wing. There was also no advertising on strips, and shirt numbers were a good thirty years away. In the meantime, the only way a 'keeper was distinguishable from his teammates was if he wore a cap on his head. Different jersey colours for 'keepers were introduced in 1909, but were only scarlet, royal blue or white at this point, with green being introduced three years later.

The ball used was rock hard, and when it got wet it could become a very heavy object that also went out of shape. Pitches suffered without adequate draining and bore no similarity to the fabulous billiard-like surfaces of the modern era. They had little grass on them, especially in the winter. Heavy rain brought puddles for the players to overcome, and on particularly rainy days the middle of the pitch would soon resemble a mud bath. This made it essential for teams to get the ball out to their wingers to attack the full-backs.

Players' boots – largely adapted from workmen's boots – were designed for strength, with a permanent, indestructible block toe and studs hammered into the soles. Given the equipment then, some of the play exhibited by the early giants of League football was extraordinary.

Initially, team formations had been entirely attack-minded, with just two defenders and eight forwards, the aim being to rush forward with the ball. Individualism was the key. Match reports from the first international game between Scotland and England in 1872 contain no reference to passing.

While it is the Scottish side Queen's Park who are believed to have been the first to recognise the value of 'letting the ball do the work', it is Preston North End, as winners of the first two Division One championships in 1888/89 and 1889/90, who are credited with refining the passing game.

This brought with it the need to adopt team formations for both attack and defence, leading to the increasing familiar 2-3-5 set up of two full-backs, three half-backs and five forwards, which dominated team formations in 1907.

The key player in a side tended to be the centre-half, who would be expected to surge ahead in support of his forwards, and it was usual for most sides to play their best, most creative player in this key position. It wasn't until 1925 that the role of the centre-half changed, when the offside rule was altered so that players could now be onside if there were only two players between themselves and their opponents' goal rather than three. This resulted in a more defensive centre-half being preferred by managers.

There were other significant differences in 1907. Goalkeepers were allowed to handle (bounce) the ball anywhere in their own half. If that made it easier for the men between the sticks, what didn't was the rule that allowed them to be shoulder charged – even when holding the ball – just like any other player. The men between the posts also enjoyed no additional protection when faced with crosses, and as a result there were some very heavy challenges in this period of the game. A keeper was however able to pick up a back pass without his side conceding a free-kick.

Bookings and dismissals were much less frequent in 1907, and in the absence of yellow and red cards it was often difficult for spectators to be sure when a player was being booked. There was no such thing as 'Fergie time', as referees rarely added on additional time unless there was a serious injury to a player.

At the start of the 1907/08 season, Newcastle United were the reigning League champions, Nottingham Forest and Chelsea had replaced Derby County and Stoke City in Division One, and The (Sheffield) Wednesday were the FA Cup holders.

Why Saturday Afternoon?

Football League rules in 1907 stated that the season was to start no earlier than 1 September, which was a Thursday that year. The vast majority of matches took place on a Saturday, with a handful of midweek games taking place in the early and later parts of the season when lighter nights – there were, of course, no floodlights at this time – meant the games could kick-off in the early evening when the aim was to attract supporters finishing work. Where games were forced to kick-off at mid-afternoon during the week, then gates naturally fell dramatically due to the fact that most people were still at work.

The day of the week, starting time and period of the year were all-important for football. The importance of religion in everyday life at the time the game made its initial few steps during the second half of the nineteenth century was underlined in rule No. 25 of the FA. This stated that 'matches shall not be played on Sundays within the jurisdiction of the Association'. Unable to utilise the one day in the week when the vast majority of people would not be at work, the game's authorities had rightly chosen the next best day, Saturday, where, starting in the 1840s, there had been a significant number of changes in the number of hours worked by many.

Increased wages, in part the result of trade union agitation, especially among industrial workers, meant that in Nottingham many hosiery workers had regular Saturday half-holidays in the 1880s, while in Lancashire builders stopped at 1.00 p.m.

In addition, many of the more traditional craft trades were less rigid about hours of work and workers could, if they wished, take Saturday afternoon off. All of which meant that crowds tended to be socially mixed, as was never the case for those behind the organising of football clubs; a survey of the occupation of 740 men who were directors of professional clubs from 1888 to 1915 showed an overwhelming majority were middle class.

By starting the season in September, clubs (many of which had started life sharing grounds with the local cricket club, and in the first League season of 1888/89 Accrington, Derby County and Notts County were still doing so) could be assured of a pitch on which to play on. So mid-afternoon was a tradition that largely exists to this day, in the lower Leagues at least.

3

SEPTEMBER 1907

Manchester United laid down a marker for the season by thrashing Aston Villa 4-1 away in the first match of the 1907/08 season. The game was played before a crowd of 20,000, and under the newly introduced rule whereby a player could now only be offside in his opponent's half rather than anywhere on the pitch. The sides were as follows:

Aston Villa: Cooch, Miles, Riley, J. Logan, Buckley, Codling, Wallace, Chapel, Hampton, Bache, Hall.

Manchester United: Moger, Dick Holden, Burgess, Duckworth, Roberts, Bell, Meredith, Bannister, Menzies, A. Turnbull, Wall.

Almost from the moment the game kicked off, Manchester United demonstrated that they were going to be serious challengers for the First Division title. Quite simply, Ernest Mangnall's side was much too good for a Villa side that was expected to challenge for the title themselves. The *Manchester Courier* headline summed it up perfectly: 'Manchester United in brilliant form.' The report said that, 'by defeating the Villa by four goals to one, United accomplished one of the best performances since the club was formed'.

It took only 4 minutes for the away team to take the lead through Wall, who received the ball from Bannister before beating the 'keeper from just inside the penalty area

It was something of a miracle that as half-time approached the score remained just a single goal to United. But when Villa's right-half Chris Buckley suffered the misfortune of breaking his ankle, the reduction of the home side to just ten men was simply too much, and Meredith scored almost immediately to make it 2-0 at half-time.

It was Meredith who scored the third goal, converting Wall's accurate cross, as the visitors continued to have all the serious play. Turnbull then had a second effort disallowed for offside before Villa reduced the arrears with 10 minutes of the match remaining.

Roberts was adjudged to have handled the ball and Joseph 'Harry' Hampton, scorer of both Villa's goals at the 1904/05 FA Cup final when Newcastle United were beaten, scored from the resulting penalty. A strong, forceful and determined player, Hampton was the idol of the Villa Park faithful and formed a lethal partnership with Joe Bache. Both men played in the 1904/05 and 1912/13 FA Cup finals and collected second winners' medals when Sunderland were beaten 1-0 in the latter.

Hampton scored a total of 242 goals for Villa, and Bache 184. Hampton was particularly noted for being able to barge goalkeepers and the ball (if he had it in his possession) into the back of the net. The men were key players when Villa won the League in 1908/09.

Roused by conceding a goal, Manchester United pushed forward and Bannister pushed the ball home on 88 minutes to give the score line a more accurate reflection. Afterwards, the *Manchester Courier* was full of praise for the whole team but singled out Roberts for particular praise while reporting that 'the 18,000 people who saw the game gave the Manchester men a capital reception as they left the field'.

'Mancunian', in the *Cricket and Football Field*, meanwhile wrote, 'That our halves were brilliant is proved by the complete failure of the opposing front rank and anything better than the play of Duckworth-Roberts-Bell – it would not be fair to divide them – would be hard to find.' Such comments would become a familiar theme over the following seasons.

Following their opening-day success, there was a good crowd of 24,000 for the first home game of the season against neighbours Liverpool. At the end of the 1893/94 season, Liverpool had beaten the then Newton Heath 2-0 at Ewood Park to take the Manchester side's place in Division One. Unlike Manchester United, Liverpool had already tasted success in the top flight, with two championship successes in the 1900/01 and 1905/06 seasons.

The game took place at Bank Street, Clayton. This was Newton Heath/Manchester United's second ground, and they occupied it from June 1893 until moving to Old Trafford in February 1910.

By 1907, Bank Street had undergone considerable improvements; its capacity had risen to 50,000 although only 5,000 or 7,000 actually watched the final First Division fixture there on 22 January 1910.

Bank Street was squeezed in among densely populated, cheaply constructed terraced housing, from which many of the club's working-class supporters would have been drawn. Children of all ages would kick a makeshift ball around on cobbled streets where the arrival of a motorcar would have been a cause of great fascination.

The ground was set among factories with belching chimneys. Charles Dickens had used Manchester as the scene for his 1854 novel *Hard Times,* and over the next fifty years numerous writers commented on Manchester's 'smoky holes' with a mixture of fear and fascination.

By the end of the nineteenth century, civic, industrial and commercial buildings had replaced most of the middle-class residential areas of Manchester city centre, with the residents leaving for estates on the outskirts of the city. Clearing the slums was undertaken with much less haste, and was to be piecemeal until the 1919 Addison Housing Act, which aimed to provide 'homes for heroes' as soldiers returned from the First World War. It was not until Rowland Nicholas' City of Manchester Plan in 1945 that things radically changed in terms of comprehensive development to redesign a largely unplanned and unregulated Victorian city.

The site is now occupied by the car park of the Manchester Velodrome, with a plaque on a nearby house wall indicating the presence of the former ground.

Manchester United's second consecutive four goals in a match saw them thrash Liverpool. Afterwards, the *Manchester Courier* gave the following verdict:

> Opinion was freely expressed by such judges of the game that no honour is too high for the team to achieve. Certainly the way in which the players have acquitted themselves so far lead one to expect great things from them this season.

In the circumstances, the Liverpool side did well to hold the hosts until Alex 'Sandy' Turnbull scored his first goal of the season with a right foot shot on 33 minutes. After that, it was simply a matter of how many goals Manchester United would get, and it would have been a lot more than four if the Liverpool side hadn't contained such a fine 'keeper as Sam Hardy. Born in Chesterfield, he had played for his home team before being signed in May 1905 by the Anfield side. He was to become a major star, bagging a League winners' medal at the end of his first season. Hardy, who played twenty-one times for England, is rightly regarded as one of the finest 'keepers of all time.

The loud cheers for both groups of players when they emerged from the tunnel prior to kick-off was an indication of a healthy away support. When Roberts won the toss, he chose to kick with the breeze and Menzies headed narrowly wide in the first minute. Hardy then produced a brilliant save to deny Sandy Turnbull. However, the 'keeper was powerless to prevent Meredith and Turnbull combining for the first goal. Wall scored the second just before the break after Turnbull's run had split the Liverpool defence, and when he pulled the ball back, the United outside-left hit a sweet half-volley. In the second half, Turnbull completed his hat-trick with two headers, both from Wall's corners.

Having played two and won two, Manchester United faced Middlesbrough home and away in consecutive weekends. The result was to be 2-1 successes for the respective home sides. At Bank Street, Manchester United was pinned back from the start of the game, and would have fallen behind if a lesser 'keeper than Moger had been in goal.

Former Derby County favourite Steve Bloomer was considered by Frederick Wall, the FA president, to be the best goal scorer he had ever seen: 'He was a great marksmen, and his splendid passes were generally made with one touch.' (*Sir Frederick Wall: 50 Years of Football 1884–1934*). Now playing for Middlesbrough, Bloomer was guilty of a poor miss just before the interval when he failed to hit the target from close-in. Bloomer is one of only two players who have finished as top scorer in the top flight of English football on four occasions, Arsenal's Thierry Henry being the other. Jimmy Greaves finished top on six occasions, twice with Chelsea and four times with Spurs.

In the second half, Wall, escaping the Boro defenders for once, hit a powerful shot that crashed back off the bar. But this misfortune seemed to inspire the Manchester United side.

Tim Williamson was in fine form in the Boro goal, but he could do nothing with a fast high drive by Turnbull, his fourth goal of the season. Ten minutes later, the same player made it 2-0, but in truth he couldn't miss after Meredith tore down the wing, ran past the

Boro defence and curled back a cross that his colleague simply had to get his head to for the ball to enter the net. Towards the end, the away side got the goal their play deserved when Bill Brawn's shot across the goal was turned in by Fred Wilcox.

Victory put Manchester United top of the League table, but a week later came the first defeat of the season. The match had opened with both sides on top, but came to life when Meredith's drive beat Williamson only to flash behind off the top of the bar. The home crowd then screamed for a penalty when Roberts appeared to handle a John Harkins drive before Brawn might have scored with a close-range header. Wilcox was then unlucky to see his header hit the bar, but the Boro man was not to be denied on 35 minutes when, after beating Holden, he scored from close range.

A minute later, Sam Aitken scored one of the best goals ever seen at Ayresome Park during its long history, firing an unstoppable shot from 40 yards past Moger, to the delight of the crowd. The development of professional football in Middlesbrough was made possible by the industrialisation of the Teesside town, where the number of inhabitants grew from just 6,000 in 1841 to 105,000 in 1911. In 1850, England and Wales had just 148 cities with over 10,000 inhabitants, and this figure had risen to 356 in 1890. The total urban population in England and Wales jumped from 20.3 per cent in 1800 to 61.9 per cent by 1890.

The development of the iron and steel trade – for many years Teesside set the world price for both – saw many large shipyards constructed along the Tees, and the crowd that witnessed the match against Manchester United would have contained many of these workers. They would have worked a half-day before grabbing a bite to eat and, hopefully, a pint, before dashing along to the match.

Two-nil down at half-time, United showed they were far from finished when Roberts skimmed the bar with a speculative effort before Williamson – Middlesbrough's all-time record appearance holder with over 600 first team appearances – made a great save from Wall, the United outside-left's only real contribution in the 90 minutes.

Although Bannister did reduce the arrears with 15 minutes remaining, Middlesbrough, with Williamson superb, hung on to avenge the previous weekend's defeat.

4

TEN IN A ROW

Defeat at Middlesbrough was to be followed by a magnificent run of ten consecutive League victories by Ernest Mangnall's side. In seven of these games, Manchester United scored four goals. At St James' Park the League champions, Newcastle United, were thrashed 6-1 in what was then the finest performance of any Manchester United side since the club's formation in 1878.

It was all the more surprising, therefore, when Manchester United crashed out of the Lancashire Senior Cup. After beating Manchester City and Bury, they were beaten 3-1 in the semi-final by Oldham Athletic. Two of the victor's goals were scored by Frank Hesham. He was later killed on active service with the Royal Garrison Artillery Regiment in France on 17 November 1915. He is buried in La Clytte Military Cemetery in Heuvelland, West-Vlaanderen in Belgium.

Later in the season, Manchester United enjoyed more success in the Manchester Senior Cup when, after beating Manchester City and Stockport County, Bannister scored the only goal against Bury in the final played at Hyde Road. United were also to win the Manchester Senior Cup in 1910.

The fifth League match of the season saw Sheffield United make the short trip across the Pennines. With Bell fully fit, he replaced Ernest Thomson at left-half. This gave supporters a chance to compare the Scottish international with the Sheffield player in the same position, Ernest Needham. The England international was in the twilight of his career in which he had captained Sheffield United to the League championship in 1897/98 and the FA Cup in 1902. Needham was also a fine cricketer playing for Derbyshire in the County Championship, scoring 6,550 runs before he retired in 1922.

The match was watched by a healthy crowd of 25,000, and throughout the 1907/08 season Manchester United's average gate was to rise from 20,695 in 1906/07 to 22,315. This was to place United as the fourth best supported club in the country, behind top-placed Chelsea (31,695), Newcastle United (27,875) and Manchester City (23,225). Only once – in 1894/95 – had United enjoyed a higher average gate than their neighbour City.

The game was a hard fought affair. It left the away side feeling aggrieved after they were denied an early golden opportunity when the referee, Mr Green, blew for a foul by Burgess on Arthur Brown as the home player's challenge had, in fact, failed to halt the Sheffield forward who was shaping to beat Moger.

Turnbull's opening goal on 8 minutes came after he received the ball from Roberts and swivelled to beat Joe Leivesley with a fierce right foot shot. Sheffield equalised on 20 minutes when Burgess lost the ball and George Thompson broke away and centred for Brown (who in 1904/05 had finished as top scorer in Division One). He held off two challenges before beating Moger.

The away side was then grateful for the fine form of Lievesley in goal. He seemed determined to ensure his side made the short trip home with at least a point, making some decisive catches when the United wingers crossed and also handling a series of hard drives from the edge of the box. However, the 'keeper could do nothing to prevent Turnbull's deft touch from a Meredith cross before half-time that ultimately won the game for the home side. The Sheffield United side contained debutant Frank Levick, who later in the season broke his collarbone when playing against Newcastle United. The former electric engine cleaner was sent home to recuperate, but he later contracted pneumonia and died. *The Manchester Guardian* described him as 'one of Sheffield United's most promising players'.

With two goals, it was not surprising therefore that both the *Manchester Evening News* and the *Sheffield Independent* selected Turnbull as the outstanding forward on the field. Brown was rated not too far behind. In comparison, both papers felt that the home side's centre-forward Menzies had played poorly.

Newly promoted Chelsea was the opponent for Manchester United's sixth League match of the 1907/08 season. The match was played at Stamford Bridge, a massive auditorium purchased by

Gus Mears in 1904 with the aim of turning it into a football ground. However, when Mears approached Fulham to lease it they turned him down and he opted instead to found his own club in March 1905 that could use the stadium. When his application for Chelsea to join the Southern League was refused, he switched to the Football League and the new club was elected.

This was to act as a spur to Tottenham Hotspur and QPR to make their own, ultimately successful, applications to join the Football League with the consequent long-term decline in the importance of the Southern League.

Having failed to hit the net in five games and having seen James Turnbull score a superb goal in the Monday match against Manchester City in the Lancashire Senior Cup, Alex Menzies found himself replaced at centre-forward by the ex-Leyton man. Although Turnbull failed to net, the decision by Ernest Mangnall proved to be a wise one as the new man worked with all the other forwards and was always available for the ball.

Having beaten League champions Newcastle United 2-0 just five days previously, Chelsea were in a confident mood for a game that was played on a boiling hot day in which temperatures reached 38°C at one point. The large crowd were treated to a magnificent display, and showed their appreciation to the away side who they roundly applauded off the field at the end.

The star of the show was again Meredith, who was constantly fed the ball by Sandy Turnbull and Bannister. 'He certainly gave as good an exhibition of wing play as anyone could wish for,' reported the *Manchester Courier*. His second, and United's fourth, right at the end of the match was a sparking run and finish that brought the biggest and longest cheer of the match.

There was also praise in the *Manchester Evening News* for Moger who, during the times when Chelsea put pressure on the United goal, showed some confident handling of the ball. Bell also received praise but it was a fine team effort all round, leading the *Manchester Courier* reporter to end his match report with the following: 'The men, extremely capable individually, have developed into an extremely formidable side now that they have become thoroughly acquainted with each other's play.'

United took the lead on 10 minutes when Chelsea foolishly left Meredith unattended to beat full-back Bob Mackie, and he hit a low drive that Jack Whitley was powerless to stop. The home side did manage to equalise when, from a corner, George Hilsdon – who later in the season scored six times against Worksop Town in the first round of the FA Cup – headed past Moger. Hilsdon, capped eight times by England, was to be badly affected by mustard gas during the First World War, but recovered sufficiently to play for Chatham and Gillingham once football resumed.

A lovely drive from Sandy Turnbull restored the United lead before, in the 48th minute, Bannister knocked a Wall cross into an unguarded net from just 3 yards out. The match was long over as a contest when Meredith scored in the last minute.

Nottingham Forest, the 1906/07 Division Two champions, arrived at Bank Street in early October 1907 for their first appearance there since they played Newton Heath in September 1893. That match ended 1-1, leaving Heath on five points from their first four games of the season and in ninth place in the sixteen-team table. It was a decent start and augured well for a better season after they had only just avoided relegation at the end of the previous season by beating Small Heath (now Birmingham City) in the Test Match play-offs that had been introduced to decide promotion and relegation. Newton Heath had finished bottom of Division One, with just eighteen points from thirty games.

In fact, the 1893/94 season was to be a disaster and, following the draw with Forest, Heath went on a run where they won two and lost fourteen of their next sixteen League games. Heath ended the season in bottom place and again faced playing in the Test Matches. This time, there was no reprieve as they lost 2-0 to Liverpool and were relegated. It wasn't until the end of the 1905/06 season that Manchester United emerged back into Division One, just as Forest experienced the drop.

Although the home side again won convincingly 4-0, most of the crowd was left disappointed, as the Manchester side was unable to replicate its fine form of previous matches. What didn't help was the persistent rain, which reduced the ground to a mud bath in patches, and a ball that looked out of shape. Without numbers on the players' backs, many spectators also found it difficult to work out which player was which.

The away side had clearly earmarked Meredith as the man to watch, and he was rarely left without two players close by. The United players did the sensible thing and used the additional space left vacant by his watching defenders, with the United attacking play being switched to the left, and Wall scoring a good goal, the third of the match. There was also joy for home debutant Jimmy Turnbull who got his first goal for the club, reward for a fine performance that drew praise from the reporter in *Athletic News*, who said, 'Turnbull showed cleverness with the ball was quick and shot with strength. He adds weight to the line and looks like keeping his place in the team.'

The home side had opened the scoring on just 10 minutes with a shot from 15 yards by Bannister. Forest fell further behind when Jack Armstrong, the Forest left-half, totally mistimed his attempted clearance from the edge of the penalty area and sent the ball flashing past Linacre for a remarkable own goal. The match was overseen by Thomas Armitt from Leek, the last referee from the League's first season in 1888/89.

Saturday 12 October 1907
St James' Park   Attendance 25,000
Newcastle United 1 (McWilliam) Manchester United 6 (Wall 2, Meredith, Roberts, A. Turnbull, J. Turnbull)
Newcastle United: Lawrence, McCombie, Carr, McWilliam, Veitch, Willis, Gardner, Speedie, Hall, Orr, G. Hedley.
Manchester United: Moger, Holden, George Stacey (debut match), Duckworth, Roberts, Bell, Meredith, Bannister, J. Turnbull, A. Turnbull, Wall.

This was, at the time, Manchester United's finest 90 minutes of football. Newcastle was the current League champion and had thrashed Manchester United, Meredith and all, at home in the previous season 5-0, as well as winning at Bank Street 3-1 at Christmas 1906. The home side, it was true, had not started the current campaign in particularly good form, but before kick-off were still not too far behind the League leaders in seventh place with just four points less.

Both sides included debutants, with George Hedley at outside-left for the home team and George Stacey replacing Burgess, who had been called upon to play at nearby Roker Park, Sunderland, as part of the Football League side, which that day beat the Irish League 6-3.

Heavy rain meant that the ground at St James' Park was soft at the start. Combined with the draw of the game at Roker Park, the size of the crowd was thus reduced. Spectators witnessed Manchester United roaring into a 4th-minute lead. Bannister and

James Turnbull broke open the home defence, and when the ball reached Meredith he drilled an accurate shot from the tightest of angles into the roof of the net. It was a remarkable goal by this brilliant player. Stung by going behind, the home side rallied and Moger was forced to make a diving save from Finlay Speedie to help United retain its lead.

Disaster struck Andy McCrombie on 25 minutes when he turned Meredith's cross into the path of James Turnbull, who made it 2-0. With the home defence now in disarray, David Willis foolishly handled in the box soon after and Sandy Turnbull scored from the spot to make it 3-0.

Hedley did his best to get a goal back but found Moger in fine form. Newcastle had to thank their 'keeper, Jimmy Lawrence, for preventing Wall making it 4-0 just before the break. Lawrence had twice played for Newcastle in the FA Cup final, but had finished with a loser's medal on both occasions in 1905 and 1906, and was to suffer the same fate at the end of the 1907/08 season and much later in 1911. He did, however, collect a winners' medal in 1910 when Newcastle beat Barnsley after a replay in the final. Newcastle captain Colin Veitch – a gifted, politically aware scholar who counted among his friends the Irish playwright George Bernard Shaw – and Jock Rutherford also achieved similar feats for the Geordies.

Five minutes into the second period, and any hopes the home fans might have entertained of a famous comeback disappeared when Wall got the goal his play deserved, driving the ball past an unsighted Lawrence from the edge of the penalty area. The keeper had only to wait another minute to concede a fifth when Roberts, dashing forward, received a square ball from Meredith before advancing to smash it home from 20 yards. In an ideal world, United's sixth would have been scored by Bannister so that all five forwards had scored, but it was Wall who made it 6-0 by sweeping home a Meredith cross, the home defence by now totally ragged. Near the very end of the game, Peter McWilliam did manage to pull a goal back with a good shot after a dribbling run, but it was a well-beaten, if not slaughtered, Newcastle side that ran off at the end.

Every single Manchester United player had played magnificently, and Newcastle had suffered their biggest-ever home defeat. Despite their obvious disappointment, the large crowd knew they had witnessed a remarkable performance and they cheered the away side from the pitch at the end.

The *Manchester Evening News* reported as follows:

> The Manchester triumph was the result of skill, and it is a long while since the defence of Lawrence, McCombie and Carr was so completely outwitted. The Manchester men are to be complimented upon a performance which will stand out as one of the achievements of the season.

Manchester United continued their impressive form the following weekend by beating Blackburn Rovers 5-1 at Ewood Park. The Blackburn side at the time was captained by the finest player ever to represent the East Lancashire club.

Locally born right-back Bob Crompton played for Rovers throughout his whole career and ended up making 528 appearances in a career shortened by the First World War. Although solidly built, he was not typical of the bruising defenders of his time and was a master tactician.

He made his debut in 1897 as a seventeen year old, and five years later was picked to play for England against Wales in the Home Championship. It was to be the first of forty-one caps for his country, a record that stood until well after the Second World War. Considering that there were at the time only three regular international games per season, the modern-day equivalent would be over 100 caps.

Crompton captained his country on twenty-two occasions. He won two League winners' medals in the 1911/12 and 1913/14 seasons. He later managed Rovers as they won the FA Cup for a then record-equalling (with Aston Villa) sixth time by beating Huddersfield 3-1 at Wembley in 1928.

The Sunderland and Arsenal legend Charlie Buchan later wrote of Crompton that he was 'the finest footballer in the world before the First World War'.

Crompton may have been a fine footballer, but not even a man of his many talents could prevent a rampant Manchester United side thrashing his charges in October 1907. It may have been 5-1, but 10-1 would not have been an injustice. The *Lancashire Evening Telegraph*, which still covers goings on across East Lancashire, said the following:

> They are the most effective combination that has been seen on the Ewood Ground for a good many years. There may have been visitors

more beautiful to behold, but I cannot recollect a team that backed
up clever midfield play with such deadliness in front of goal.

The away side's crucial second goal was the pick of the bunch,
Meredith showing pace and trickery to bamboozle the Blackburn
backs before crossing to Sandy Turnbull who, hurling himself
forward, headed the ball from little more than a foot off the ground
past Willie McIver in the Rovers goal. Wall wasn't to be outdone,
however, and later, after leaving Crompton trailing in his wake, he
whipped over a cross that left Jimmy Turnbull with the simple task
of heading into the net for United's fourth goal.

It had taken the away side just 10 minutes to open the scoring
before a crowd of 27,400, Rovers' largest crowd of the season who
paid a total of £897 for the privilege. On a soft ground, Duckworth
received the ball near the halfway line and, after beating Arthur
Cowell, ran down the wing before finding Sandy Turnbull, who
drove the ball past the Rovers 'keeper.

Rovers equalised 10 minutes later when Bill 'Tinker' Davies
curled the ball away from Moger. But when United regained the
lead with just 5 minutes of the first half remaining, the knowledge
that they would be playing with a strong breeze in the second half
must have given Mangnall's men real confidence.

It was therefore no great surprise when Meredith teed Sandy
Turnbull up for the third, and it was from another Meredith floated
cross that the same man scored his third goal and the away side's fifth.

The *Athletic News* was succinct when it summed up the away
side's performance: 'Manchester United were splendid everywhere',
and 'the best feature was their half-back line-up.' Roberts was
singled out as the best player for the winning team, who were now
hot favourites to win the League.

Yet, despite such a heavy defeat, the *Athletic News* selected
Crompton as the best player, stating, 'his greatness was plain to see
and I cannot help but wondering [sic] what would have happened
if the England captain had not been playing for Rovers.'

Bolton Play Just Three Men Up Front

In the tenth match of the 1907/08 season, Manchester United
played Bolton Wanderers before a Bank Street crowd of 35,000.
This game was unusual because of the decision of Bolton manager

John Sumerville to adopt a cautious approach. Wanderers were in the middle of a spell where they were too good for Division Two but not good enough for the top flight, having gone down in 1898/99 and 1902/03, only to be promoted in 1899/1900 and 1904/05. They were to be relegated at the end of the 1907/08 season, before returning as Division Two champions the following season, only to go down again in 1909/10 before returning once again in 1910/11.

In parallel with modern-day football, where visiting sides to Old Trafford often set out with only one man up front, Bolton, defying the traditions of the day, adopted a defensive approach by playing 'only' three up front. The change had the desired effect of preventing a rout, and Bolton were never out of contention as a result. The away side even levelled when, on 33 minutes, Holden made a mess of his clearance and John Boyd took advantage to score with a fierce drive.

Sandy Turnbull had opened the scoring with a darting, jinking run from 35 yards before beating 'keeper John Edmundson from 6 yards.

The winning goal was even better. Burgess blocked a Bolton attack to feed Bannister, whose ball inside released Jimmy Turnbull, and his mazy 40-yard run helped create the space for a wonderful curling goal. The victorious side left the field with a five-point lead at the top of the table.

Manchester United's great run continued when it faced Birmingham (City only being added to the club's name in 1943) at St Andrews. With the home side struggling at the bottom of the League, the news that William Henry 'Billy' Jones was fit enough to play after a lengthy absence due to injury was a big boost. He was a popular player with the Birmingham fans, earning the nickname of the 'Tipton Smasher' for scoring over 100 goals in just over 250 appearances at the club in two spells between 1901/09 and 1912/13.

With the home half-backs finding it difficult to keep pace with the United forwards, it was no great surprise when the League leaders struck on 15 minutes, James Turnbull driving the ball home. Thoughts that this might lead to another United rout was quickly dispelled when almost from the kick-off Billy Peplow crossed for Jones to head the equaliser. Five minutes later, Manchester United was back in the lead when Meredith nipped between Frank Cornon and Frank Stokes and, from a narrow angle, beat Nat Robinson with a powerful drive. Birmingham was level within 2 minutes, Ninty Eyre heading home, and at half-time the score remained 2-2.

In the 55th minute, Meredith again broke through the home defence to make it 3-2. Two minutes, later Duckworth passed to Wall, who from 12 yards out made it 4-2. In the 89th minute, Birmingham, who had never stopped trying, reduced the arrears when Eyre scored his second goal of the match.

Despite seven goals being scored, the *Athletic News* was full of praise for both 'keepers, who they felt had performed admirably. Meredith was seen as the best player overall, although Jones was also lavishly praised. Both teams were cheered as they left the pitch.

Seven goals were also scored in the following weekend's game during a match that was one of the finest ever seen at Bank Street, and in which Manchester United just edged out Everton 4-3. The latter were a fine side, and on a soft, slippery surface they were first into their stride, Alex Young and Jimmy Settle both firing shots narrowly wide. The Merseyside team was also not without aggression, and their rough tactics were to eventually lead to captain William Balmer being spoken to by the referee in the first half. The Everton right-back was, however, unable to do anything when Meredith slipped past him to give Billy Scott no chance for the game's opening goal.

As had happened at Birmingham the previous week, United conceded an equaliser within 60 seconds. It came when Hugh Bolton and Settle broke through, leaving the former to score on 30 minutes.

Roberts gave the home side an early second-half lead when he headed home a Meredith corner, and the Welshman then twice broke beyond the Everton backs to pull the ball back for Wall to crash home two goals. It was enough for the reporter in the *Manchester Courier* to report, 'Meredith emphasises each week that he is the greatest player of this or any age.'

Everton, 4-1 down, were stung and with 5 minutes left, Settle made it 4-2. Two minutes later, Moger dropped the ball and it was pushed home by Settle. With United pushed back, there was panic in the defence. Moger atoned for his earlier mistake when he dived bravely to prevent an equaliser from Harry Makepeace, a player who is unique in the world of sport as he is the only man to win an FA Cup and League championship winners' medal (both with Everton), be capped as a soccer international (with England four times), win a County Cricket Championship medal (with Lancashire on four occasions) and be capped as a cricket international (four England caps versus Australia in 1920/21).

With eight consecutive League victories, the question was 'who will stop Manchester United?' The next to try were Sunderland, four-time League champions. The Sunderland side contained the former United man Bonthron, who was unfortunate enough to put the ball into his own net when a greasy ball spooned off his toe for what proved to be the winning goal in a tight match.

United's 2-1 away success owed much to some fine goalkeeping by Moger and the defensive play of Roberts in front of him. Sunderland was unlucky at the start of the game, when Billy Hogg's shot beat Moger but flashed off the top of the crossbar and into the crowd behind. The United 'keeper then saved twice from Arthur Bridgett, an England international who scored England's first goal on an overseas tour when he netted in Vienna in a 6-1 defeat of Austria on 6 June 1908.

With the ground packed out well in advance of the advertised kick-off time, the game started 20 minutes early. On 15 minutes, Hogg raced through onto a pass from Sam Raybould. His shot was good but Moger made a good save. Jimmy Raine then volleyed in a shot that went at a tremendous pace and looked like beating Moger, until the custodian leapt to deflect the ball past the post. As the interval approached, a feature of the United defence was the superb form of Roberts, who artfully checked the home forwards.

Sunderland finally grabbed the lead their play deserved when James Turnbull made a mess of a header and sent the ball past his own defenders for Raybould to race through and score.

However, within a couple of minutes, Meredith turned Henry Low and squared the ball for A. Turnbull to equalise with a header. There was now greater variety and pace in United's moves, and when A. Turnbull centred, Bonthron unluckily pushed the ball into his own goal.

The visiting full-backs and Moger successfully resisted a supreme effort by the Roker forwards in the last 25 minutes, and Sunderland left the field beaten rather unluckily. The official return showed that 30,852 people passed through the turnstiles with the record receipts being no less than £1,050 4s 3d. A tenth of this, or £105 12s, was given to the town of Sunderland's distress fund.

Manchester United completed the first ten-match-winning run in the top flight of English football in the club's history when they beat Woolwich Arsenal 4-2 at home on 23 November 1907. The game was marvellous entertainment for a rain-soaked crowd of

10,000 on a pitch that, long before the end, was little more than a mud bath, particularly down the middle of the field. Arsenal were behind within 2 minutes when Jimmy Ashcroft was beaten by Sandy Turnbull's low drive, but the 'keeper then kept his side in the game with a fine save from a Roberts shot. On 32 minutes, the League leaders made it 2-0 – James Turnbull missed Billy Meredith's cross, but his goal-scoring colleague Sandy Turnbull was on hand to push the ball home.

On 55 minutes, the away side were back in the game when William Garbutt tricked Burgess and beat Moger (who, like Ashcroft in the opposite goal, was now ankle deep in mud) from 20 yards. Two minutes later, the United 'keeper dropped a David Neave highball. Peter Kyle (who during his football career played for, among others, Liverpool, Leicester City, West Ham, Spurs, Arsenal, Aston Villa and Sheffield United) was on hand to push it home to make it 2-2. Was Manchester United going to drop its first point since way back in August? The answer was no.

United regained the lead from a great Sandy Turnbull header following a curling cross into the box from Duckworth (who as a youngster had worked as a moulder before turning professional with Newton Heath Athletic for a weekly wage of 7s 6d – 37.5p). Mangnall paid a transfer fee of £50 for him in October 1903 and he made his official debut, after his first appearance was in an abandoned match at Grimsby, in the match against Gainsborough Trinity on 19 December 1903, playing at centre-forward, he scored. He became a right-half when he volunteered to play there at short notice in a reserve derby match with City on 25 December 1903. However, it was not until the 1906/07 season that he established himself in the first team.

Turnbull's goal brought scenes of great rejoicing among the home crowd, and they were even happier when, following an Archibald Gray miskick, Harry Williams pulled the ball back for Sandy Turnbull to score United's, and his, fourth goal of the game, making it 4-2.

Afterwards, the newspaper reports praised both sides for producing such a fine display, and although Sandy Turnbull was clearly the Man of the Match with four goals, there was great praise for the United half-back line-up, with 'Mancunian' in *Sport and Field* stating, 'it was where the game was won.'

5

FIGHTING FOR THEIR RIGHTS – THE PLAYERS' UNION

Manchester United's remarkable run to the top of Division One didn't necessarily mean the players were happy with their lot. Like many other professional footballers, they were angered by the maximum wage limit that restricted their earnings to just £4 a week, even though gates were booming. They were also concerned about the way clubs treated their players and could recall that when Jimmy Ross, the Preston North End, Liverpool and Manchester City legendary scorer, had been forced to retire early on ill-health grounds (that ultimately led to his death at just thirty-six in 1902), he had been unable to save any money for his wife and children.

Then, on Monday 8 April 1907, Thomas Blackstock, a Manchester United reserve full-back with thirty-eight first-team appearances since his move to the club from Cowdenbeath in June 1903, died during the course of a Lancashire Combination fixture against St Helens Recs. Blackstock collapsed during the first half of the match and his teammates were outraged when they entered the dressing room at the interval and discovered he had already been transported to the Mill Street mortuary. The player had played on the Saturday and had not been selected for the Monday early evening match but had turned up wanting to play. At the subsequent inquest into Blackstock's death, a verdict of 'natural causes' was returned and his family was to receive no compensation, a fate also experienced by the family of Manchester City's left-back David Jones, who died during a pre-season game in 1902, leaving the club to claim he had not been 'working' at the time.

On 22 December 1897, the *Lancashire Daily Post* announced, 'Football professionals form a union. An ambitious scheme floated.' Among those participating were Jimmy Ross and his Preston colleague Bob Holmes, John Devey of Aston Villa, and John Cameron and Jack Bell of Everton, with the union to be called the Association Footballers' Union (AFU).

Central to their demands was for negotiations regarding transfers to be between the interested club and the player concerned, rather than between the clubs with the player excluded. The players' struggle suffered a serious setback when several players were lured by the higher wages then on offer in the Southern League, with Cameron joining Tottenham Hotspur and leading them to FA Cup success in 1901.

Negotiations with the Football League thus ended in failure and in May 1900, the FA's AGM agreed to set a maximum wage for professional footballers in the Football League at just £4 a week. This was less than many of the top players were receiving but in excess of what the majority of players earned. Many leading League clubs ignored the rules and continued to pay higher wages by utilising under-the-counter payments. At least seven clubs were investigated and punished for 'financial irregularities' between 1901 and 1911, and in November 1905, Middlesbrough were fined £250 for creating fictitious accounts and eleven of twelve directors were suspended until 1 January 1908.

It was against this background that several of the players at Manchester United, including Charlie Roberts, Herbert Burgess, Sandy Turnbull, Charlie Sagar, Herbert Broomfield and Billy Meredith set out to form a new Players' Union. The first meeting was held on 2 December 1907 at the Imperial Hotel, Manchester. Meredith chaired the meeting that was attended by around 500 professional footballers, and the Association Football Players' Union (AFPU) was formed. There was the briefest of reports in some of the following day's national papers.

Trade union membership had risen from 2.2 million in 1906 to 2.5 million by the end of 1907. It was to go on rising over the next few years and reached 4.1 million just before the start of the First World War.

Meredith used his weekly column in the popular *Weekly News* to argue the case for the union, saying in one article, 'The players are, as a whole, an over-generous race who do not heed the morrow or prepare for a rainy day as the wise men would. This trait in the character of the players has been taken advantage over and over again by club secretaries in England.' The Welshman argued that 'in an uncertain career why should a footballer not have the best money that he can earn?' It was the issue of pay and the altering of the maximum wage that was seen as a priority for the emerging union.

Meredith had worked as a miner until he was twenty. In 1893/94, he was locked out by the employers in a struggle over wages, and the national dispute was only resolved when the government (for the first time ever in an industrial dispute) intervened to settle the affair due to their concerns about the detrimental effect on the economy from a shortage of coal.

Two weeks after the northern meeting, Meredith chaired the London meeting that was held at the Charterhouse Hotel. The first management committee meeting was held in January 1908, and consisted of three Manchester United players – Meredith, Broomfield and Roberts – who were joined by Harold Mainman of Notts County, Walter Bull of Tottenham Hotspur, Andy McCombie of Newcastle United, Bert Lipsham of Sheffield United and C. J. Craig of Bradford City. A request to the FA for a fundraising meeting was granted, and this was held at St James' Park after the competitive season ended when Newcastle took on Manchester United.

The new union announced its first objective in the following press release:

> To promote and protect the interests of the members by endeavouring to come to amicable arrangements with the governing football authorities with a view to abolishing all restrictions which affect the social and financial position of players and to safeguard their rights at all times.

The union would help transfer-listed players find employment, provide temporary financial assistance for those in need and generally regulate relations between players and their employers. The union would also provide its members – who paid a 5s entrance fee (25 pence) and subs of 6d (2.5 pence) a week – with legal advice.

In 1906, the Workmen's Compensation Act paved the way for all workers to obtain compensation for injury at work. While the new union was keen to take cases to court to establish that players were working men, the FA insisted – and has done to this day – that all disputes should be resolved internally. When proposals from Broomfield supporting the establishment of a claims board consisting of union reps and club members were dismissed, tensions between players and clubs increased.

In August 1908, offices were opened in St Peter's Square, Manchester, and were staffed by newly appointed secretary Harry Broomfield, who by this time had joined Manchester City.

Although most clubs were happy to maintain the £4 ceiling on wages, the larger ones would have been happy to scrap it as they could have then lured the better players to play for them. As Manchester United was now one of these clubs, it was hardly surprising that, initially at least, both the club's owner, John Henry Davies, and president, John J. Bentley, backed the players' campaign. John Lewis – referee, militant abstainer who often denounced the evils of drink, founder of Blackburn Rovers and Football League committee member – was also supportive.

All were to subsequently change their attitudes. In December 1908, C. E. Sutcliffe – the leading member of the Football League management committee – viciously attacked the Players' Union's 'amazing proposals'.

The Burnley director who, during his time on the committee, was responsible for working out the details of the four League expansion programmes – in 1898, 1905, 1919 and 1920–23 – that together raised the League from thirty-two to eighty-eight clubs, was perhaps considering his own club's position. He must have recognised that if clubs with larger gates were free to pay higher wages, then inevitably they would be able to attract the better players and the smaller clubs like Burnley would suffer. Many directors of other clubs would have no doubt considered the possibility of similar problems if the Players' Union were successful in having the maximum wage scrapped.

Sutcliffe's argument, though, was subtle. He denounced the players' proposals on the grounds that they would lead back to the days 'when a spirit of selfishness was ruining the game and the clubs'. During the 1880s, many professional players were attacked for being mercenaries for moving from club to club in their dash to obtain better wages. Sutcliffe deliberately ignored the fact that it had been the clubs themselves that had encouraged such behaviour. His prejudice thus launched the fight back to the clubs against the players. It was sufficient to create a split in their union, with the more moderate leading players, such as Newcastle's Colin Veitch, keen to demonstrate a more 'responsible' attitude to negotiations.

The union could certainly have done with a good negotiator, as Meredith would then surely not have been allowed to go ahead with a light-hearted article in January 1909, in which he fantasised about players going on strike. This allowed the likes of Sutcliffe and Bentley to take the moral high ground and paved the way for the popular press to raise concerns that the new union was set to ask England players not to play for their country against Scotland. Once the strike bogey was out of the box it was difficult to put back, and with a large number of players indicating they were not with the union. It led to England captain Bob Crompton using his after-match dinner speech following the Scotland game to attack the organisation.

When the Players' Union discussed joining the General Federation of Trade Unions (GFTU), the fact that it was formed independently of the Trades Union Congress to promote industrial peace and to seek to prevent strikes was deliberately ignored by those now so opposed to the Players' Union within the Football Authorities. They seized on the possibility that in the event of a general strike, the GFTU would support it and instruct footballers to do the same.

Having undercut the credibility of the Players' Union, the FA then withdrew recognition and suspended its chairman and secretary, Mainman and Broomfield (who were both already in effect non-players), and all players were told to resign from the union by 1 July 1909 or be sacked for their clubs. The players now had to decide whether they were prepared to take strike action and fight for improved wages and conditions, as there was no way they were going to get them under their current arrangements with the clubs and the FA. The Players' Union affiliated to the GFTU on 1 July, but when Broomfield toured the country to speak to players, he found that few were willing to stand their ground and the majority were prepared to resign from the union in order to continue playing.

Broomfield had hoped to persuade players not to play on the opening day of the 1909/10 season, but it quickly became clear he was facing an uphill struggle. Charlie Roberts was the first to declare he was unwilling to sacrifice his principles, and he was quickly joined by other Manchester United stars who, on turning up to collect their summer pay, were sent packing without it and barred from Bank Street.

The United men decided to do their pre-season training at Fallowfield, site of the 1893 FA Cup final and home to Manchester Athletic Club. Newspaper reporters, keen for a story as ever, arrived to interview and photograph the rebels. Alert to some good publicity, Roberts helped create a legend when he obtained a piece of wood and wrote on it 'Outcasts Football Club 1909'.

The photograph subsequently appeared in many newspapers the following day, and would clearly have annoyed the players' opponents. The actions of the players forced the FA to act, and on 4 August 1909, the organisation requested a meeting with the GFTU. This went badly, but by mid-August it was announced that players from Newcastle United, Sunderland, Oldham, Liverpool and Everton were backing their colleagues at Manchester United.

On 18 August 1909, an under-pressure FA met the Players' Union executive for the first time since they had ended recognition and even agreed to sign a joint agreement sanctioning further discussions, in which the FA would pursue abolition of the maximum wage and the retain-and-transfer system that tied players, with or without their agreement, to their clubs. It was a declaration that promised much but committed the footballing authorities to nothing in particular.

A week later, the FA representatives then refused to sanction payment of just £38 in lost summer wages for all players who had not left the union by 1 July and, in effect, had been sacked for not doing so. Meredith was convinced it was the FA's way of getting out of a settlement, as there was 'no doubt that the FA and the clubs believed that, if put to the test, the players would not fight'.

The FA were to be proved right. Over the following days, in the lead-up to the start of the season on 1 September, a shabby compromise agreement was to be negotiated under the direction of Colin Veitch. Following a meeting in Birmingham on 31 August that was attended by 100 players – but not Roberts, Broomfield or Meredith – the Newcastle player agreed to personally try and secure a settlement in which, in return for the FA agreeing to recognise the union and its legal right to represent members in court, and also pay summer back pay, there would be no strike. The players present backed such a proposal and Veitch dashed off to persuade – successfully – the suspended Manchester United players to play in the following day's game against Bradford City on Thursday 1 September 1909.

Broomfield was 'not overjoyed at the agreement and Meredith felt that the FA had only recognised the union if the players observe the rules and practice of the FA. What's the good of belonging to a union if one fetters one's hands like that?' Veitch was at odds with his Manchester colleagues, stating there had been 'Peace with Honour ... and a gigantic leap'.

The United side wore Players' Union armbands the following day and when they emerged on to the pitch, it was clear that the vast majority of the crowd had supported their actions, as the cheers they received were louder than usual.

It was to take six months for the players' back wages to be paid. Charlie Roberts also had his benefit match against League champions Newcastle refused. Benefit matches were one of the few legal methods by which a player could boost his income. At the discretion of the club and FA, he could keep the receipts of a selected match. In the event, Roberts' benefit match over Christmas was well supported. With Veitch taking a leading role in negotiations, there were few concessions granted to the players as the maximum wage was increased to £5 for the start of the 1910/11 season. The FA demanded the union end their affiliation with the GFTU, even though ending membership still did not prevent players taking strike action if they so desired in the event of a general strike. Union members backed the FA voting 470 to 172, and in December 1909 Broomfield quit his post.

Meredith, knowing that the maximum wage and the retain and transfer system were to remain in place, made it clear that footballers had lost the struggle. The Welshman told the papers, 'The unfortunate thing is that so many players refuse to take things seriously but are content to live a kind of schoolboy life and to do just what they are told ... instead of thinking and acting for himself and his class.'

It was to be many, many years before footballers were to get the rewards they were entitled to, and although those Manchester United players who led the way in the early twentieth century were allowed to continue playing, they never received the rewards their talents deserved.

6

RUNAWAY
LEADERS PEGGED BACK

It was the Wednesday (Sheffield only being incorporated into the club's name in 1929) who ended Manchester United's winning streak before a then record Hillsborough attendance of 40,000 (38,397 plus ticket holders). Sheffield as a city had developed enormously during the nineteenth century, when the population rose from 60,000 to 451,000, many of whom were housed in back-to-back dwellings. George Orwell later described Sheffield as 'the ugliest town in the Old World'.

On two previous occasions, the Wednesday had been successful in winning the First Division title in 1902/03 and 1903/04, and now there were hopes of a third. They were lying in second place before the match and victory would cut United's lead to four points.

The match proved worthy of such a fine crowd, and few, including a great many from Manchester who saw it, would have left disappointed by the entertainment on offer. It was the away side that was the better of the two sides on show in the first half, with Meredith constantly threatening to get beyond the home defence. On more than one occasion, Jack Lyall in the home goal produced a superb save, with both Turnbulls, Wall and Meredith all denied at various points during the first 45 minutes.

Things also looked bleak for the home side, which consisted for the first time of the XI that had beaten Everton in the Cup final the previous April, when it became clear that the side's playmaker at centre-half (Tom Crawshaw) was only fit enough to limp out the match on the far right. Crawshaw was Wednesday's captain and a ten-time England international. His injury, at age thirty-five, proved difficult to overcome and he retired soon afterwards.

The reshuffle in the home defence saw little Harry Chapman move back from his outside-right position to play centre-half. Chapman – whose brother Herbert is arguably English football's greatest-ever manager, with success at Huddersfield Town in the 1920s and Arsenal in the 1930s – had a fine match and was to show great versatility. With Billy Bartlett finally getting to grips with Meredith, Manchester United was proving second best as the crowd roared on Wednesday. And it was Bartlett who opened the scoring with a shot that left Moger helpless.

The away side thought they should have had a penalty shortly afterwards, but the referee, Mr Pearson of Crewe, decided that Harry Burton had not handled. The United players, disappointment increased when Burgess was ruled to have handled a George Simpson effort, but Moger kept his side in the contest with a fine save from the resulting penalty from Tom Brittleton. However, the Manchester United 'keeper was subsequently given no chance when Andrew Wilson, for once escaping Robert's attention, forced an opening for Jimmy Stewart, scorer of the opening goal at the 1907 FA Cup final, to drive his side into an unassailable 2-0 lead. Not that the side had played badly, with the *Sheffield Independent*'s reporter at the match commenting afterwards, 'A very fine all round side are Manchester United; and despite their failure to get through Saturday's great ordeal successfully, they will probably win the League championship all the same.'

The sixteenth League match of the 1907/08 season resulted in a 2-1 win for United at home to Bristol City. The visitors arrived on the back of an easy home victory against Nottingham Forest by three goals to nil, a result that had taken the Robins up to fourth place in the table but nine points behind the leaders. The teams played in front of a sparse crowd on a pitch almost totally devoid of grass, which quickly became a mud bath after persistent overnight rain.

Late spectators would have missed the two captains needing three attempts to decide the toss after the coin of the referee, Mr J. Mason of Burslem, twice became stuck in the mud. It was not the most auspicious of starts. Especially as, just prior to kick-off, a strong wind had also decided to make an appearance, which Bristol City were asked to kick into after Roberts eventually won the toss.

There was an early surprise after the away side took the lead when Holden made a mess of his clearance and left Frank Hilton with a simple chance. There was even an opportunity for a second when Hilton was clean through, but just as he went to shoot, Duckworth dived in bravely to force the ball to safety.

The equaliser came from another brilliant goal by Meredith. As City pushed up the field, he used his pace in a driving run that ended with him flashing the ball past George Lewis before crashing into the post and having to be revived by the United trainer Fred Bacon. On his return, the Welshman was given a tremendous ovation from the crowd and showed he was far from finished by hitting another shot just wide. Lewis then kept the scores level with a great save from Jimmy Turnbull and at half-time the score stood at 1-1.

It should have been 2-1 to United within seconds of the restart, but Meredith, for once, was guilty of a wild attempt on goal from just a dozen yards out. In the circumstances, it might have been better to have allowed someone else to take the penalty that the home side won, courtesy of another sparkling Wall run shortly afterwards. Meredith, however, was given the task and fired well wide.

During the interval, Wall had been presented with a magnificent bronze statue from Mr G. E. Howarth in recognition of having taken part in fifty successive League games. With 10 minutes of the game remaining, the winger produced a sparkling winner when he dribbled the ball across the box before hitting a fine shot that the Bristol keeper could only watch whistle by.

There was a trip to the cricket ground for the next League encounter for Manchester United. Formed in 1862, Notts County are the oldest professional League club in the world, and when Manchester United travelled to play them in December 1907, they faced a club that was among the original twelve Football League members in 1888. County played their homes games at Trent Bridge County Cricket Ground, not moving to their current ground Meadow Lane until September 1910. The County side in 1907 was selected by members of the board of directors. This was common with many other Football League clubs at the time.

In goal for County was Albert Iremonger, who was well known for his outspoken nature on the football pitch. The 'keeper would often leave his goalmouth to argue decisions made by match officials, sometimes situated in the centre of the pitch. He still holds the record for the most appearances for Notts County at 601, of which thirty-seven were in the FA Cup. Iremonger also played County Cricket for Nottinghamshire from 1906 to 1910.

The County full-backs were Herbert Morley and John Montgomery. The latter had been sent off twice in 1907, first against Stoke on 19 January and then against Birmingham on 9 February. However, it was the former who proved the real villain in the history of football as he, along with Newcastle United's Bill McCracken, helped pioneer the offside trap that angered many spectators who objected to its success on the grounds, saying it was unsporting.

As was the custom of the day, Notts County, on winning the toss, elected to play with the wind. Despite this, the away side played better, more effective football in the first 45 minutes and, with 5 minutes remaining, Meredith gave Manchester United the lead when he collected a Roberts pass and scored a great goal with a left foot shot.

Another win was very much on the cards, and it appeared certain when Meredith's shot appeared to be grabbed from behind the line by Iremonger on 55 minutes; however, the referee was unable to say for certain it had crossed the line and County survived. Two minutes later, the home side equalised when Walter Tarplin created an opening for Fred Jones to beat Moger. This was to mark the start of County's best spell of the game, with dependable wingman Jerry Dean, who later emigrated to Canada, giving Burgess and Bell down the United left a torrid time as County searched for the winner.

In the first decade of the new century, 3,150,000 people emigrated from Britain and Ireland, up by a million on the last decade but 100,000 fewer than between 1881 and 1890. From 1871 to 1911, 10.4 million emigrated in all, around a third of the total for the world of 32.8 million. Most people (around 20.5 million) emigrated to the USA, with Argentina/Brazil at 6.15 million in second place. Those who moved often hoped to escape poverty at home, and many were assisted with transport costs by their respective governments, with some even purchasing land for migrants.

The final score of 1-1 meant it was a happy United squad that departed for two weeks special training on the sands at Norbreck, returning to Manchester for the derby match with City on the Saturday before Christmas. This attracted a crowd of 35,000 to Bank Street for a sensational match.

The sides lined up as follows:

Manchester United: Moger, Holden, Burgess, Duckworth, Roberts, Bell, Meredith, Bannister, J. Turnbull, A. Turnbull, Wall.

Manchester City: Smith, Hill, Norgrove, Buchan, Eadie, Blair, Dorsett, Wood, Thornley, Jones, Conlin.

Both teams received the cheers of their supporters when they ran onto the pitch for a keenly awaited match. Despite the already intense rivalry between the two clubs, previous games between them had been relatively free of ill feeling. However, there was to be little indication of the 'season of goodwill' on show on this particular occasion. Sandy Turnbull was to become the first player to be sent off in a Manchester derby, although afterwards there was considerable criticism of George Dorsett for falling over so theatrically when it appeared that he had received only the slightest of flicks from the United man's outstretched arm on his neck in the 55th minute of the match.

The City man later told reporters the blow had chopped off his wind, which was reported in the *Manchester Courier* as at least 'explaining what appeared to be a silly attempt on the part of the City player to make the assault look a bad one'. Not everyone at the match might have agreed, but the incident had the effect of turning an already rough game into a brawl for the next 10 minutes before both sets of players saw sense and settled back down to play football.

The state of the pitch was poor at the start and got worse as the game progressed, with the final stages being played on a mud bath. United, however, showed themselves to be a far superior side, adapting to the conditions almost from the off and employing their wingmen throughout to great effect. Meredith appeared to have been singled out for special attention as according to the *Manchester Courier* match report he 'got more hard knocks than he has received for some time'. The ex-City man, though, was to have the last laugh, playing a part in two of the home side's three goals.

The League leaders had taken the lead through Wall, who, following up a fine double save by Walter Smith from Meredith and Sandy Turnbull, found the net with a shot that must have hurt the 'keeper, as it went in off the side of his face.

Despite pushing forward, City only once seemed likely to fashion an equaliser, but John Wood was guilty of a bad miss after Jimmy Conlin's ball had split the United rearguard. It was therefore no great surprise when Sandy Turnbull headed home a Meredith free kick to make it 2-0. With half-time approaching, Billy 'Lot' Jones and Conlin, who, despite being an Englishman, enlisted with the 15th Battalion of the Highland Light Infantry as a private when the First World War commenced and was killed at Flanders on 23 June 1917, missed decent opportunities to send their team in just a goal down.

The contest was over within minutes of the second half getting underway, when Frank Norgrove was dispossessed by Sandy Turnbull, who scored his second goal of the game to make it 3-0. City was down but they then managed to pull a goal back when Bill Eadie headed home from a corner.

Just 10 minutes after Turnbull's dismissal, Burgess limped off with an injury likely to keep him out of the side for the next few matches, and the way seemed open for City to grab a point. It was at this point that the United defence of Moger, Holden, Roberts, Bell and Duckworth dug deep, playing the final 24 minutes of the game as though their very existence depended on winning the match. When the referee blew the final whistle, Manchester United had won a famous match by beating their neighbours 3-1.

In light Sandy Turnbull's sending off and the unpleasant incidents that followed, referee Mr F. J. Wall's match report to the FA was later released to the newspapers. He made the following comment:

In the first half I had occasion to warn and then caution Turnbull upon his conduct, and in the second half he struck Dorsett of Manchester City in the face with the back of his hand. I at once ordered him off. The blow was certainly a mild one and undoubtedly Turnbull received provocation from the attitude Dorsett took up but in the face of the previous caution I had no option. I regret that for some little time after the players on both sides appeared to lose their heads and indulged in childish and irresponsible tactics that to say the least of it, were anything but creditable to them and yet not of sufficient character to enable me to carry out the greater powers invested in me.

P. J. Wall, Esq, FA, 22 December 1907

In the following days, the newspapers saw fit to run a series of cartoon drawings on events at Bank Street, with the *Manchester Courier* showing a retreating, bedraggled City army, two sets of players engaging in arm-to-arm combat in the middle of the field and, finally, one of Dorsett falling theatrically with the referee rushing to send Turnbull from the field. Turnbull would now have to go before the FA Committee who would decide on whether to suspend him.

A crowd of 45,000 saw Manchester United take on near neighbours and title rivals Bury on Christmas Day in 1907.

Today, of course, there would be no prospect of sides playing on 25 December. Yet it was only at the end of the 1956/57 season that a full Football League programme on Christmas Day was ended. In 1965, Blackpool and Blackburn played the last-ever Christmas Day fixture in England, with Blackpool winning 4-2.

Unlike their near neighbours, Bury had previously captured a major trophy by winning the FA Cup in 1900 and 1903, creating a record score in the latter match when they beat Derby County 6-0.

With Burgess' thigh not having recovered from an injury sustained during the City game, there was a recall for Stacey at left-back. Bury manager Archie Montgomery, a former United 'keeper and brother of Notts County full-back John, meanwhile decided to replace Joe Leeming at full-back with Johnny McMahon, who it was felt was better placed to combat Meredith. It did not prove to be the case.

Although the away side started brightly, it was the home side who went into the interval with a two-goal lead. Wall created the first with a wonderful cross that Jimmy Turnbull nodded home, and just before half-time the United winger squared a lovely ball to Meredith who, taking the ball in his stride, hit it back across the goal and into the net off the post with James Raeside well beaten.

Bury was determined to get itself back into the game once it restarted, and it pressed the home XI back towards its own goal. Peter Gildea seemed to be everywhere, dashing down one wing and then the other, shooting on sight and inspiring his colleagues. The goal Bury deserved duly arrived, although it would be disallowed as, after Moger caught a dropping cross, he was shoulder-charged by Kay; he dropped the ball and, after it was pushed back into the middle, Bob Currie got the final touch.

The goal inspired Bury, but standing in the way of the team's efforts were Holden and Stacey, who both defended magnificently. Pushed back, United hung on to claim both points after Moger made a series of fine saves to deny a Bury side that left the field feeling aggrieved that their efforts had failed to earn, at least, a point.

The two sides met again seven days later, before which United had taken a point in a 0-0 draw at Deepdale, where both they and Preston failed to excite the crowd. A near miss by Meredith in the first half was the only real effort on goal, and the entertainment on offer was poor fare for a Christmas crowd. The point earned meant that in 1907, the away side had played a total of thirty-seven League games, winning twenty-seven, drawing four and losing six;

if maintained in 1908, this form was certain to see the First Division trophy on display at Bank Street at the end of the season.

First Division League Table on 28 December 1907

	Games Played	Points
Man Utd	20	34
(Home: 10-0-0, 29-11; Away: 6-2-2, 27-13)		
Newcastle	21	25
The Wednesday	20	24
Bury	21	24
Bristol City	21	23
Everton	20	22
Aston Villa	21	21
Notts County	23	21
Woolwich Arsenal	20	20
Preston North End	21	20
Chelsea	21	19
Liverpool	19	18
Sheffield United	19	17
Bolton Wanderers	19	17
Blackburn Rovers	20	17
Middlesbrough	21	17
Nottingham Forest	20	16
Birmingham	21	16
Sunderland	21	15

Manchester United was nine points clear at the top with eighteen matches of the season remaining; could they capture their first major title in 1908?

Both Bury and Manchester United were unchanged from the Christmas Day fixture and, as expected, there was a large crowd for the New Year's Day tussle, with Gigg Lane being packed to the rafters well before kick-off.

Although the weather was remarkably sunny for the first day of the year, it was accompanied by a cold, biting and blustery wind that threatened to spoil the game.

Having won the toss, Bury captain Jack Dewhurst chose to set his opponents to face the wind. It didn't take too long for the first opportunity when a Stacey clearance lacked distance, but Bury inside-right Bob Currie shot wide. Billy Hibbert, the home centre-forward, was then denied by a clever interception by Roberts, whose wonderful pass out to the left would have sent Wall away dangerously if Dewhurst hadn't upended him for a free-kick. Wall then reversed the play by hitting the ball over to the right to Meredith, whose shot seemed about to reach Sandy Turnbull in front of goal before James Raeside dashed out to grab the ball.

Ernest Mangnall's side continued to press and Raeside was forced to push away a shot from Wall, before Bury swept forward and Roberts showed the defensive side of his game by heading away a cross when the ball was swept into the United box. This marked the start of some considerable pressure from Bury. It looked like the home side had made the breakthrough when Hibbert, who twice in the previous game at Bank Street had seen his shots beat Moger only to end up stuck in the mud, headed Peter Gildea's cross past Moger only to see the linesman's flag go up for offside. Manchester United were then similarly disappointed when Roberts headed back Wall's corner, and when Meredith hit a hard shot, James Turnbull's turning of the ball into the net brought the raising of the linesman's flag.

Wall then brought gasps of appreciation from the crowd. Advancing with the ball, he seemed to weave between Dewhurst and Jimmy Lindsay, the only Bury player remaining from the famous FA Cup final-winning side of 1903, only to let himself down by subsequently pushing the ball too far in front of the United forwards advancing towards the Bury goal.

The United left-winger, however, was having one of his best games for the club and for a while the ball seemed to be stuck to his foot, as pass after pass was sent in his direction. Lindsay, the Bury right-back, would no doubt have liked to kick him out of the ground, but he couldn't get near him to do so. Lindsay was one of the earliest goal-scoring full-backs in the history of the game, his accuracy from the penalty spot allowing him to net twenty-nine goals before he retired in 1909.

Considering how windy the conditions were, the game was a fine, exciting affair that remained goalless at the interval. Within seconds of the restart it really should have been 1-0 to the League leaders when, following a Hibbert miskick, Roberts sent Wall away. When he pulled the ball back across the goal, the United forwards seemed uncertain who should take it on and the chance was wasted.

Wall, however, was not going to be denied forever. On the hour mark he got the goal that he deserved. Bannister dashed through and when his shot was fumbled by the 'keeper, Wall was on hand to knock the ball into the net.

Within seconds of the restart, Roberts was badly injured and had to be assisted from the field to receive treatment. Duckworth was asked to fill-in for the centre-half, with Bannister dropping to right-half. Although United were forced to play a man down for the remaining 30 minutes, they did so without any serious problems. When the referee blew the final whistle, they had won a tough game 1-0 at the ground of one of their closest rivals for the title.

It seemed nothing was going to stop Manchester United winning their first-ever Division One trophy. That was the case even after a weakened side was beaten 2-0 in the following League match away to Sheffield United, whose Bramall Lane ground is the oldest major ground anywhere in the world, having hosted its first game in 1862 – a match between Hallam and Sheffield Club. Bramall Lane also hosted the world's first-ever floodlit football match on 14 October 1878, with two teams picked from the Sheffield Football Association. The power for the lights was provided by two generators.

Kerr Whiteside made his only first-team Manchester United appearance at Bramall Lane in January 1908, replacing an injured Duckworth at right-half. With Charles McGillvray making only his second appearance and first in the League at centre-half, it was clearly going to be a difficult time for the former Scottish Junior International signed from Irvine Victoria in May 1907.

For the home side there was a debut for James Hobson, signed from Worksop. He must have feared the worst when North, one of his colleagues at centre-half, was hurt early on and absent from the pitch for much of the following proceedings. With ten men, it was remarkable that a Sheffield side lying just outside the relegation zone became the first to beat the runaway leaders since their near neighbours the Wednesday had done so in November.

Manchester United was unlucky not to take the lead in the first minute but Wall's shot came back into play from the crossbar. Sheffield then scored with their first attack, Arthur Brown's powerful run leaving William Batty with a chance from 12 yards that Moger had no opportunity to save. When North was carried off, Brown was forced to drop to centre-half, from where he continued to pull the Manchester United defence to pieces with a series of darting runs forward and passes to his forwards.

The match appeared to have been decided when, following a corner kick at the beginning of the second half, Willie Wilkinson hit a shot that Moger, with players in front of him, only saw once the ball had entered the net. This seemed to rouse the away team and Wall was unlucky when he hit the woodwork twice with the 'keeper beaten. With Meredith for once kept quiet by the excellent Needham, the League leaders were unable to exert sufficient pressure on Joe Lievesley in goal to reduce the arrears, and when the game ended the home supporters in a 17,000-strong crowd were overjoyed.

There was sympathy in the *Manchester Evening News* for both Whiteside and McGillvray: 'It would be most unfair to blame the reserve men for the defeat', especially as Whiteside had clearly been injured early the second half. By comparison, the *Sheffield Independent* felt that 'Roberts and Duckworth were badly missed', especially as Whiteside had been unable to give 'Meredith the sort of support which the famous right-winger is accustomed to receive from Duckworth'.

The result and performance had been a poor one for Ernest Mangnall's team, and while Wall, Holden and Moger in goal had all performed with distinction, that wasn't the case for the team as a whole who, according to the *Sheffield Independent*, had 'given little evidence of that greatness which has given them their proud position at the head of the League'.

Chelsea travelled north to face Manchester United at Bank Street for the first time on 25 January 1908. Ten days earlier in London, Robert Baden-Powell, famous for organising the successful defence in the Siege of Mafeking, which lasted from October 1899 to May 1900, started the publication of the *Scouting for Boys* handbook. The book – revised on more than thirty occasions – has gone on to sell over 100 million copies and it effectively began the worldwide Boy Scout movement.

Following the ease with which the Sheffield United forwards had run through the United half-back line the previous weekend, Ernest Mangnall was prepared to gamble by allowing Roberts, who had turned up expecting only to watch, to play in this match although he was clearly not fully fit.

The manager's need for a player such as Roberts was the result of the absence of some key players. Firstly, Duckworth had been ill during the week and it was felt unfair to play him as he was due to play for the North in a match against the South at Hyde Road the following Monday – the England that would play against Ireland in February would be selected from this match. In the event, the United player may have been wise not to have played in the game as his was a lethargic performance in a match that finished 4-4 and Derby County's Ben Warren retained his place at right-half in the England side for the Home Internationals.

Duckworth never did represent his country, although he did play five times for the Football League and was included on a FA Tour Party to South Africa in 1910. In this respect, Duckworth would certainly challenge Steve Bruce for the winner of the best United half-back never to play for his country award.

Up front against Chelsea, Sandy Turnbull was unavailable after being suspended by the FA for one game as punishment for his sending off against Manchester City in December. Bannister also had to call off playing at the last moment owing to the death of his mother.

The manager decided that there was to be no second chance for Whiteside as there was a long-awaited return for Alex Downie, who had been a mainstay in the side until Duckworth had finally made the right-half place his own in the previous season. Jack Picken was selected as Bannister's replacement and Menzies played for Sandy Turnbull in a match that turned out to be his last for Manchester United.

Since the earlier fixture in the season at Stamford Bridge, the Chelsea side had been strengthened by the signing of William Brawn from Middlesbrough for £950 in November. He had a powerful shot and was unusually tall for a winger at 6 foot 2 inches. He played twice for England and collected an FA Cup winners' medal with Aston Villa in 1905.

The match was a very poor affair, one easily forgotten by the crowd of around 20,000, and afterwards the *Manchester Evening News* was especially critical of the forwards:

> Not one of the ten players did themselves justice, the six inside (inside, right-centre, forward-inside, left) men in particular were poor in the extreme. When Menzies changed places with Picken there was a big improvement, the only decent forward play of the match being seen during the last fifteen minutes.

Indeed, it was during this time that the only goal of the game arrived when James Turnbull found himself unmarked with the ball at his feet and drove it past Jack Whitley. The Chelsea 'keeper might have been beaten earlier when the home side were awarded a penalty after John 'Jock' Cameron handled the ball, but Wall drove his shot straight at Whitley, who saved easily.

The League leaders faced the League champions on 8 February 1908, and after Manchester and Newcastle United drew 1-1, the *Manchester Evening News* asked whether a 'better exhibition of football has ever been witnessed at Clayton'. Second-placed Newcastle had lost just the once in its sixteen previous League and Cup matches, and was determined to ensure there was no repeat of the St James' Park thumping earlier in the season.

The match was watched by a Bank Street record crowd, many of whom had gained entry for free after climbing into the ground, and after just 6 minutes, the game had to be stopped when one section of the overcrowded ground spilled over the barriers and onto the pitch. In fact, it was something of a miracle that the game ever reached its conclusion, or that no one was seriously injured.

When the game restarted, Manchester United pushed back the League champions. Downie, filling in for Roberts, who had returned to the side too early after an injury, had a fine game at centre-half and was constantly finding his forwards with some wonderful passes. It was Sandy Turnbull, however, who was responsible for picking open the Newcastle defence for the opening goal, sending James Turnbull running onto a delightful through ball. With the Newcastle defenders appealing for offside, the United striker beat the advancing Dick Pudan to the ball before firing into the open net to the delight of the huge crowd. It might have been 2-0 at half-time, but the United scorer was just too slow to react to a loose ball only seconds before the referee blew the whistle to end proceedings.

When the game resumed, it was clear that Newcastle was going to do everything in its powers to avoid defeat and, if possible, win the match. No side had so far even taken a single point away from Bank Street; could Newcastle be the first? An equaliser looked absolutely certain when Peter McWilliam was presented with the ball just 6 yards out but, with only Moger to beat, he fired well wide.

By now, the home side was constantly pressed back, but in Burgess they had the best player on the field, and time after time he blocked the away side's forwards as they shaped to shoot.

With 10 minutes left, it looked as if Manchester United were going to hang on for a famous victory, one that would put them well on course for a first-ever Division One title, but then Alex Gardner's free-kick to the back of the penalty area was headed back across by Bill Appleyard for Jimmy Howie to tap home and make it 1-1. With the home team literally on its knees, it was not a question of whether they would suffer the loss of their first home point so far this season, but whether they could hang on for a draw.

With 5 minutes of the match remaining, Appleyard, a 14-stone battler nicknamed 'Cockles' – he was a former North Sea fisherman – seemed to have the game won for Newcastle, brushing past Burgess and firing a low drive that Moger spilled. As the ball moved to roll over the line, the 'keeper made a desperate recovering save to ensure the glorious game ended 1-1.

Along with Burgess, Bell had also played magnificently while on the Newcastle side. Joe Ridley's pace had been a constant threat, but all the forwards on both sides had played well.

After such a fine display, the next match at home to Blackburn Rovers appeared a formality. Manchester United was unbeaten at home and Rovers had not won away all season. When the two teams had met earlier in the season, Rovers had been thrashed 5-1 and had also failed to win in ten games. To make matters worse, the team was going to have to make do without its captain and best player Crompton, on duty for England against Ireland in Belfast for the opening match of the Home International Championships. This was a match the away side won 3-1.

The match had been declared by the United Committee as a benefit for two of the team's stalwarts; Bell, playing in the game, and Downie, who was not on display as Roberts was back at centre-half. The two players would have much preferred the Sunderland, Chelsea or Newcastle game for such an occasion, as the match was expected to attract fewer people than for those occasions. This was in fact what happened, with just 15,000 at Bank Street, and turnstile receipts of just £298. Both players were reported afterwards to be 'greatly upset', although there was some consolation for the pair when United later obtained permission from the FA to increase the benefit money paid to each of them to £250.

With George Wall on international duty for England, there was a debut – and in the event, only game – for Tommy Wilson at left-wing.

The match proved to be an odd affair, with the home side enjoying the majority of possession and plenty of opportunities in front of goal. Yet at the end, few of those present would have begrudged a hard-working, talented Rovers side their victory, as after they took the lead they rarely looked like surrendering it. When the away side's defence was breached, it was from the penalty spot.

Walter Aitkenhead had put Blackburn ahead in the 20th minute when Billy Bradshaw broke forward and, on a pitch partly covered with water, was able to get to the byeline before crossing to find Aitkenhead. The Blackburn lead was doubled just a minute into the second when, after John Martin, Ernest Bracegirdle and Bill Davies linked up, the latter beat Moger with a crisp shot.

United got back into the game when, following a handling offence by Albert Walmsley in the 75th minute, Sandy Turnbull struck the resulting penalty past Willie McIver. However, the 'keeper was determined not to be beaten again and twice in the last 10 minutes he made outstanding saves to deny both James and Sandy Turnbull.

The result pushed Rovers out of the relegation zone, but with Newcastle only able to draw at home to Manchester City, and third-placed Wednesday heavily beaten by Aston Villa, it meant United's lead at the top remained a healthy six points with two games in hand. The result was a little reminder however that the League trophy was not yet at Bank Street.

Despite the defeat, Manchester United's commanding lead in the League meant there were hopes that they might emulate Preston North End in 1888/89 and Aston Villa in 1896/97 by becoming the first side in the twentieth century to record the coveted League and FA Cup double. United disposed of Second Division Blackpool at home by three goals to one in early January and beat Chelsea 1-0 in the second round of the FA Cup. Both games were of little quality. Not so the third match, which saw United overcome a tricky pitch and blustery conditions to win 2-0 at Villa Park and set up a quarter-final tie away at Fulham.

The Cottagers were enjoying a first season of League football after winning the Southern League in the previous two seasons. Although he did not play against Manchester United, Fulham's squad included Jimmy Hogan, who had studied as a boarder at Salford Diocesian Junior Seminary, St Bede's College, Manchester, before taking up a relatively unsuccessful career as a professional footballer. However, once he turned his hand to coaching players, his abilities shone through, though not in Britain where he was only briefly a manager with Fulham and Aston Villa in the 1930.

Before then, Hogan worked right across Europe, managing national sides in the Netherlands and Switzerland, as well as club sides that included MTK Budapest, FK Austria Vienna and RC Paris. His ideas emphasised greater control of the ball and greater movement off it. When England was thrashed 6-3 by Hungary in 1953, the president of the Hungarian Football Federation, Sandor Barcs, said afterwards, 'Jimmy Hogan taught us everything we know about football.' Matt Busby was a great fan of Hogan and felt his talents had not been properly employed in his native country.

Before a huge crowd of 41,000, Fulham created a major sensation by winning 2-1. While Bill Harrison, with his two goals, was undoubtedly the hero of the hour for the Cottagers, it was the Londoner's defence that was the major factor in their victory. Leslie Skene, in particular, had a memorable game between the posts, showing some extraordinary goalkeeping skills in the first half in particular. In the second, he was grateful to his half-back line-up in front of him, who worked tirelessly to prevent the away side creating the chances to at least force a draw.

At the same time, Fulham also enjoyed a degree of luck when Skene appeared to catch a header from Sandy Turnbull after it had crossed the line, and when Bannister's shot hit the 'keeper's legs and went behind for a corner. Fulham's opening goal was also fortunate when an attempted clearance by Burgess saw the ball cannon off Harrison and past Moger into the net in the 11th minute.

Harrison, along with Bob Dalrymple and Fred Mouncher, was a constant threat to Duckworth, Bell and Roberts. The League leaders had equalised when, on 56 minutes, Meredith seemed to be taking the ball out of play, but he hooked it back for Sandy Turnbull to head across goal where James Turnbull turned the ball home.

The winning goal came in the 65th minute when Moger was unable to prevent Harrison's shot entering the net, despite getting a hand to the ball. The Fulham man could have had a hat-trick shortly afterwards if Burgess hadn't rescued his side with a sliding tackle as he shaped to shoot.

As the game moved towards its conclusion, James Turnbull seemed certain to equalise and force the tie to a replay, but Archie

Lindsay, straining every muscle, hooked his shot over the bar. In the last few minutes, amid great excitement, Fulham hung on amid intense pressure to send their supporters home ecstatic.

The game was probably the finest that Craven Cottage had witnessed, and although the rewards for success couldn't have been greater, the match itself was played in a sporting manner that did credit to both sides. United may have lost but they emerged with their reputation intact.

Having celebrated wildly, Fulham supporters' hopes were dashed in the semi-final when Newcastle United achieved a still-to-be-broken record semi-final victory of six goals to nil. The Geordies lost to Division Two side Wolverhampton Wanderers in the final.

7

LEAGUE TITLE WRAPPED UP

Despite the Cup defeat, Manchester United was clearly intent on wrapping up the League title as soon as possible. After beating bottom-placed Birmingham City 1-0 in a poor match at Bank Street, the League leaders beat Sunderland 3-0 at home. The struggling Wearsiders arrived having recently signed 'keeper Leigh Richmond Roose from Stoke City.

Roose, whose amateur status allowed him to move between clubs, was a colleague of Meredith's in the Welsh National Team, making his debut for Wales in a 2-0 defeat of Ireland in 1900. He ended up with twenty-four caps following his final game against Scotland in 1911. Along with Meredith, Roose was one of Wales' key players when the team won the British Home International Championship for the first time in 1907.

The 'keeper had played for his country the previous weekend when they had gone down 2-1 to Scotland after taking the lead through William 'Lot' Jones. Wales had been denied the services of Meredith after the Manchester United committee, in light of the Fulham Cup match, had refused to allow him to play. English clubs at the time would often refuse to release Irish, Scots or Welsh players to play for their countries, but could not deny English players the chance to represent their countries as FA rules forbade it. Both Roose and Meredith were set to play for their country on the following Monday at the Racecourse Ground against England.

Standing 6 foot 1 inch and weighing over 13 stone, Roose was perfectly built to meet the robust strikers of the period on equal terms – comparisons with Peter Schmeichel in more modern times would not be inappropriate, especially as he was well-known for saving penalties.

Roose was noted for taking advantage of the rules in 1907/08 that allowed the goalkeeper to handle (but not hold on to) the ball anywhere in his own half. It has been said that the 1912 rule alteration, whereby a 'keeper was forbidden to handle outside the penalty area, was due to his performances.

Roose later played for Aston Villa and Arsenal, but was killed at the Battle of the Somme during the First World War in 1916. His body was never recovered and he is listed on the war memorial to missing soldiers at Thiepval. He had a fine game at Bank Street in 1908, but was powerless to prevent Bell, Berry and Wall scoring in a United side left weakened by Holden's bad knee injury in the game with Birmingham.

The full-back had played his final game of the season and, despite eventually recovering, he was never quite the same player. Fortunately, his twenty-six League appearances meant he received a League winners' medal at the season's end, something denied to him when United again won the League in 1910/11, as during that campaign he made only eight League appearances. His injury presented an opportunity for George Stacey to cement his place in the starting line-up.

Back in London, after their cup defeat at Fulham, Manchester United lost 1-0 away to Woolwich Arsenal on the Manor Field ground. Broomfield was selected to make his League debut in place of Moger, who was missing due to blood poisoning in his finger. The 'keeper had to be down smartly to save a Charlie Lewis shot as Arsenal showed their intent in the first minute of the game.

Arsenal had been founded in 1886 and was the first southern club to join the Football League. For the majority of their time in south-east London, Arsenal played at the Manor Ground in Plumstead, a three-year period at the nearby Invicta Ground between 1890 and 1893 excepted. The Manor Ground was initially just a field, until the club installed stands and terracing in time for their first Football League match in September 1893. They played their home games there for the next twenty years until moving permanently to north London in 1913, when Woolwich was dropped from the club's name.

The Arsenal manager, Phil Kelso, had clearly urged his players to get forward, and long-serving Charlie Lewis, David Neave and Harold Lee all forced Broomfield into decent saves before the

Manchester United side finally had their first effort on goal. This appeared to inspire the away team as they then dominated the rest of the first half. Wall beat the Arsenal defence for pace only to shoot narrowly wide, when he might on another day have scored. At half-time the game remained deadlocked at 0-0.

Within seconds of the restart, a driving run by Meredith, perhaps his only real contribution all afternoon, ended unluckily for the Welshman. His shot was kicked away from the line by Andy Ducat, with Ashcroft beaten. Clearly, this was not going to be Meredith's week! Arsenal too was unlucky, although when Charlie Satterthwaite, who had helped Liverpool win their first First Division League title in the 1900/01 season, hit the crossbar, it rebounded and Lewis somehow hooked the ball over the bar from just 3 yards out.

With the game by now seemingly set to end in a draw, Woolwich Arsenal managed one final attack and, from a Neave cross field pass, Lee headed the ball into the net. This prompted tremendous celebration from the home spectators in an above-average crowd.

When the referee sounded his final whistle, victory had gone to the harder working, more determined outfit on the day, and although the away side were still well in front in the League, a points total of seven from seven games was a much poorer return than in the early part of the season.

Things then got worse when the leaders travelled to Anfield for a Wednesday afternoon match that, as was to be expected on a working day, drew a lower than average crowd of just 10,000.

Having easily beaten Liverpool at home in September, and also recorded their first-ever victory at Anfield courtesy of a single Sandy Turnbull goal at the end of the previous season, table-topping United were intent on making it three wins in a row against a Liverpool side back in twelfth place and a full fourteen points behind the leaders.

However, and not for the last time in matches between Liverpool and Manchester United, the form book was torn apart and so was the Manchester United defence, especially in the first half. The match had originally been planned to take place in January, but frost had caused its postponement.

Ted Dalton made his debut for Manchester United, replacing the injured Burgess, while there were also appearances for Downie and Picken as replacements for Bell and Sandy Turnbull. At the same time, Liverpool was also forced to field a weakened side with Sam Hardy, out through a knee injury, Maurice Parry and James

Bradley's places taken by Ted Doig, Thomas Chorlton and James Harrop respectively.

The small crowd witnessed an exciting match, in which it took only 3 minutes for Liverpool to take the lead. Joe Hewitt fastened on to a centre from Goddard to crash home a magnificent shot that caught the underside of the bar before flying into the net. Nine minutes later, Billy met another Arthur Goddard cross to make it two.

Robbie Robinson then knocked home a Jack Cox cross for 3-0 before McPherson drilled in the fourth on the stroke of half-time. Manchester United had already conceded more goals in 45 minutes than in the whole 90-minute duration of any other game that season – back in 1895, Liverpool had battered Newton Heath 7-1, could they equal or even better this in 1908?

Doig, however, gave the away side a lifeline at the start of the second period, dropping Robert's free-kick to a grateful Wall to make it 4-1, and then miskicking to present the United outside-left with his and his side's second. Four-two. Was there to be a famous comeback? When McPherson made it 5-2, the answer was no, especially as Robinson then made it 6-2.

However, the away side was determined to go down fighting. Despite being four goals down, they pinned the home side back around their penalty area, with Turnbull and Bannister reducing the arrears to 6-4 with a quarter of an hour left.

It was now a game that no spectator could take their eyes off. Doig made a marvellous save from Meredith as Manchester United pressed, before Hewitt, who had been outstanding during the game, finally ended any doubts about who would win by making it 7-4. When the final whistle sounded 'the enthusiasm equalled anything seen on the ground for many a long day. Absentees may think United were not trying too hard.' They were, as *The Football Field* reported. It had been a truly marvellous match that must go down as one of the finest between the two sides.

Two days after the game, nearby Aintree witnessed a major shock in the 70th Grand National held on the famous course: 66 to 1 outsider Rubio, ridden by Henry Bletsoe, raced to victory. The horse was owned by Lord Penrhyn, whose family at one time had owned thousands of slaves on their Jamaican sugar plantations, and who was a slate quarry owner from North Wales.

Fears that Manchester United might be throwing the League title away were allayed in the following match at home to the

Wednesday, in which Ernest Mangnall's side went ahead in the first minute.

The goal scorer was debutant Harold Halse, signed for £350 from Southern League side Southend United after scoring 200 goals for the Shrimpers as a replacement for James Turnbull. It was to be the first of fifty-six goals that Halse was to score for Manchester United in 123 League and Cup appearances before he signed for Aston Villa in the summer of 1912. It may also have been his luckiest, as it came when Walter Miller, the Wednesday centre-half, in attempting to clear Halse's first shot, hit the ball off the United man only to see it loop over Jack Lyall, whose frantic efforts to retrieve the ball were in vain.

Any hopes, however, that this might be the start of a thrilling game were not fulfilled as both sides had trouble controlling the ball in windy, sunny conditions. Halse might have scored a second but with both defences well on top it was no great surprise that the score was still 1-0 at half-time.

Broomfield saved smartly when Andrew Wilson shot towards goal in the second minute of the second half. When the ball spun away it seemed certain to end up in the goal, but Duckworth timed his sliding run to perfection to clear just as Jimmy Stewart looked to prod home. A goal then might have made it an interesting game. But on 55 minutes, Manchester United doubled their lead when, following a neat interchange of passes down the right, Meredith pulled the ball back only for Bannister to totally miss it. When the Wednesday defenders failed to properly clear, Meredith again crossed and this time Wall made no mistake.

Stewart was unlucky not to reduce the arrears when his shot cannoned back into play off the foot of the post before Wilson beat Broomfield with a fine shot to make it 2-1. The away side's hopes, now raised, were soon extinguished. Within minutes, Sandy Turnbull was left unmarked to score and Wall outpaced Willie Layton to run on and beat Lyall with a well-placed shot to put the home side 4-1 up, which is how the match finished.

The result meant that Manchester United's lead at the top of the table rose to seven points with a game in hand. Eight points from eight games would be enough for Mangnall's men to win the title.

Man Utd	30	45
Newcastle United	31	38
The Wednesday	31	36

One of the necessary points came in the away game against Bristol City at Ashton Gate, where the home side was missing Billy Wedlock (who was playing that day for England at Hampden Park in the Home International Championship deciding match against Scotland).

As on many other occasions, Wedlock had been selected to play centre-half for England rather than Charlie Roberts. This upset many fans of the Manchester United player at the time, and it is generally accepted that Roberts' exclusion – he played all three matches in the 1905 Home International Championship, and never played again for his country – was because of his participation in the Players' Union. Roberts certainly had his champions, with the legendary Charlie Buchan rating him as the 'finest centre-half I have run up against ... as an all-round player, others fail into insignificance compared to him.'

In Wedlock's defence, it should be noted that Manchester United was keen for Roberts not to be picked for his country in 1906, and the Bristol City player made his England debut, before union developments, in February 1907. He was also outstanding in a narrow 1-0 victory against Ireland at Goodison Park, with the *Daily Mirror* reporting the following:

> Wedlock was, although the smallest, the most conspicuous player on the field. With eager, boyish face he fought every inch of the ground with Irish forwards, but was less clever in feeding his own boys. Still, enthusiasm counts and Wedlock can stay.

He did so for the following twenty-four matches and was to make a total of twenty-six appearances for his country.

The *Athletic News*' Tityrus selected Wedlock in his ideal team from all Englishmen, and although Sir Frederick Wall, FA secretary from 1895 to 1934, selected N. C. Bailey of Old Westminsters, he was also a big fan of Wedlock. The International Select Committee of which he was a member felt that 'Wedlock was always with the ball; its closest companion. In most matches he would play the ball thrice to the once of any other man ... he signified perpetual motion.' Because of his barrel shape, the 5-foot 4-inch tall, 11-stone Wedlock was known as 'Fatty'. In his day, he was as much a phenomenon as the recently retired 'keeper Bill 'Fatty' Foulkes.

The international match ended 1-1, with Chelsea's Jimmy Windridge equalising a first-half goal by the Wednesday's

Andy Wilson for the home side. It meant that the title was shared.
Windridge scored seven goals in eight internationals for England.
He was the cousin of Alec Leake, the Aston Villa, Burnley and
England defender.

It was lucky that the match finished as too many people had been
allowed in: the attendance of 121,452 was then a world-record
crowd. Only the intervention of the police kept the pitch clear. It
appeared that the football authorities had failed to learn the lessons
of 1902, when twenty-five fans died when part of a stand collapsed
during a Scotland-England game played at Ibrox, home of Glasgow
Rangers. With Ireland later beating Wales in the final match, the
Welsh had gone from top to bottom of the table in a year.

At Ashton Gate, Sammy Gilligan replaced Wedlock at centre-half
and after Harry Clay fisted away Meredith's shot the home side was
unlucky when William Maxwell's shot hit the upright. Pat Hanlin's
tussle with Meredith was one of the highlights of the game, but
just before the break the Welshman finally broke clear. When he
crossed, Wall hit a powerful shot that went in off the crossbar to
give Manchester United a 1-0 lead.

In the second period, the home side appeared to have had little
chance of getting back into the game, especially as Manchester
United now had the advantage of kicking with a stiff breeze behind
them. Meredith missed narrowly on two occasions before Halse's
long-range shot hit the bar.

However, with 20 minutes left, a mix-up in the United defence
saw Maxwell score the equaliser. Both sides might have welcomed
a point beforehand; City to keep them out of the bottom two and
a stuttering United, whose sparkling form in 1907 had long since
given way to ragged, hotchpotch performances, because it moved
them a point nearer the title.

Title as Good as Sewn Up
League Match 32 – Everton [A]
Wednesday 8 April 1908   Goodison Park   17,000
Everton 1 (Young), Manchester United 3 (Halse, A. Turnbull, Wall)
Half-time 0-1

When it became apparent that both Newcastle United and the
Wednesday had lost to Aston Villa and Middlesbrough respectively,

winning at Goodison Park meant that Manchester United had to all intents and purposes captured the First Division trophy for the first time in the club's history. It may have been this that inspired United when Everton equalised in the 67th minute of the match, Joe Donnachie beating Duckworth and Stacey before drawing Broomfield and squaring the ball for Alex Young to complete the formalities by pushing the ball into an empty net.

Having dominated their opponents, the injustice of conceding a goal saw the away side pour forward. When Sandy Turnbull's shot was handled by Walter Balmer, the United inside-left thrashed home the penalty to the joy of a small handful of the side's supporters who had been able to make the trip for the midweek afternoon fixture.

Halse, who was preferred to James Turnbull at centre-forward once again, had given his side the lead in the first half, surprising Billy Scott with a curling shot. It was Wall who added the third in the final minute of the match, hammering home a shot that the Everton 'keeper probably never even saw.

Meredith, Turnbull and Wall had all played magnificently, but this was a fine all-round team performance, at the end of which Manchester United rightly earned the applause of the crowd.

Table

Manchester United	32	48
Newcastle United	34	38
The Wednesday	33	38
Manchester City	33	38

Conspiracy?

League Match 33 – Notts County [H]
Saturday 11 April   Bank Street   20,000
Manchester United 0, Notts County 1 (Dodd)

Despite being assured of a first-ever League championship trophy, the Bank Street crowd were outraged at the Manchester United performance in this match. Notts County was fighting for survival and had a more than decent defence, so a hard game was assured. Before the match it had been announced that the move to the proposed new stadium in Stretford had now been agreed. While undoubtedly a sign of the club's development, this might not necessarily have been welcomed by all supporters as at least some would now have to spend much more time and expense travelling across the city if they wished to keep watching the champions.

What appears to have angered the home fans was the feeling that many of the home players hadn't tried to either win the game or entertain them. People paid good money, which they had to work hard to earn, and if they were willing to spend it on football then the least they felt they deserved was 100 per cent effort from the players, even if the team they followed had won the League!

What sparked off the sustained abuse from the crowd was when a remarkable penalty was awarded just after half-time, no Manchester United player seemed keen to take it. It had been expected that Sandy Turnbull would take the spot kick, but when he refused, later citing a couple of knocks to the head and a damaged ankle, Wall stepped forward to send the ball well wide and bring booing from the crowd.

Writing in the *Football Field* the following Saturday, the columnist named the 'Mancunian' even reported that some of the Notts County players shook hands with Wall after he missed. If true, this must give rise to the possibility that money had changed hands on the outcome of the match, as was to be the case seven years later when Manchester United played Liverpool in a relegation tussle and players from both sides won money by backing United to win 2-0.

As the game moved towards its conclusion, it became apparent that a number of the United side was apparently indifferent as to how the game would end. So when Notts scored almost on full-time, some spectators went absolutely wild with delight and heaped further abuse on the side. George Dodd had taken the ball extremely well on the run and rounded Stacey before beating Broomfield with a low shot. There was some sympathy for the 'keeper in the *Manchester Evening News* when a match report argued that neither he nor the United defenders deserved such hard luck.

The hostility from the crowd was such that many Manchester United players took much longer than usual to leave the ground, by which time they would have become aware that, with Manchester City and Sheffield Wednesday both losing, they were League champions.

The crowd's actions were subsequently the subject of much comment in many newspapers – one fan, who wrote to *Football Field* signing himself 'Play Straight', had this to say:

I am sure I am only voicing the opinion of 75 per cent of the spectators when I say that it was the most disgraceful exhibition of football that it has ever been my lot to witness between two teams. My complaint is purely and simply against the home team, who after the first 20 minutes never made an honest effort to score. Let the directors make a full and complete inquiry, and if need be get rid of the players who are to blame for I am sure the spectators would rather see a team of inferior men who played the game honestly than a lot of men who play ducks and drakes in a match.

Having captured the title, United stuttered towards the end of the season. They were beaten by Nottingham Forest at City Ground on Good Friday, when Enoch West and Tom Marrison scored for the home side in a 2-0 success. West's goal was one of twenty-eight during the season, a record that made him top scorer in the League at the end.

The champions followed this up the next day with a battling 0-0 draw before a 40,000-strong Hyde Road crowd. In this game, Walter Smith in the Manchester City goal constantly defied the attacking away forwards to earn his side a point. Unlike the earlier match at Bank Street during the season, the game was played in a decent spirit and City might have won it if George Dorsett had not headed wide when well placed with just 10 minutes left.

Two days later, Manchester United lost their second consecutive home game when Aston Villa won 2-1 at Bank Street, where the counter attraction of the Manchester races kept the crowd to below 10,000 to watch a match played in bitterly cold conditions.

Villa was ahead on 3 minutes after Alf Hall beat Duckworth with a lovely feint before hitting a shot that flashed just inside the post. It was a great goal. The League champions were level on 15 minutes when Meredith's ball to Picken was knocked past George. Joe Bache threatened to restore the away side's lead as the game moved from one end of the pitch to the other.

United then suffered a blow when James Turnbull was so badly injured he had to see out the rest of the game at outside-left. Just before half-time, Hall should have made it 2-1 to Aston Villa but hit a low shot just wide of the post. The Villa forward was not to be denied however, and in the second half scored his second, and the match-winning goal, from the penalty spot. Broomfield got his hands to the spot kick but just failed to prevent the ball entering

the net. With two goals, Hall had been the Man of a very fine
Match to help give Villa five wins out of six games, and when it
became six from seven, five days later, the Birmingham side ended
up as runners-up to Manchester United in the League at the end
of the season.

Manchester United played their fourth game in six days when
they faced Bolton Wanderers for a midweek fixture at Burnden
Park. Four goals were shared in what was a poor match. Bolton
were also guilty of failing to take advantage of a weakened side.
Leading 2-1, the relegation-threatened side sat back and conceded
a late equaliser when Stacey converted a penalty with 10 minutes
remaining after Meredith had been brought down in the area by
Boyd. As a consequence, the draw left Bolton needing a point against
relegation rivals Notts County the following Saturday to guarantee
Division One safety. Manchester United meanwhile needed to beat
Preston North End to break Liverpool and Newcastle United's
record points total of fifty-one, recorded in 1901 and 1907.

There was a League debut for Aaron Hulme in the final League
match of the 1907/08 season, while United fans were pleased to
see Moger return to the side in goal after a number of weeks out
with injury.

There was a big cheer for Hulme when, with his first touch in
League football, he headed clear as Dickie Bond shaped to head
home a first-minute goal. Strong pressure from the home side then
saw Wall hit the post before Charlie Dawson headed narrowly wide
for Preston.

Billy Lyon, playing at right-half for Preston, found himself the
object of the referee's displeasure shortly afterwards, a series of rough
challenges earning him a booking. After this, he reacted childishly
for a considerable period of the game, refusing to participate in the
match or respond when the ball was played to him. His behaviour
may have contributed to his side falling behind when, after Billy
Meredith broke through and shot, Tommy Rodway turned the ball
past his own 'keeper Peter McBride.

Preston's 'keeper then kept his side in the contest with a fine
save from Bell before a remarkable goal for Preston, although
the shot wasn't anything special – Moger might have stopped it
on another day. Lyon had once again been persuaded to take part
in proceedings, and with his first touch he hit a free-kick into the
United net to make the score 1-1 at the interval.

When play resumed, Wall and Thomson both had shots charged down before Halse hit a piledriver that almost broke the crossbar. The unlucky Halse was in scoring mood though, and he headed home a Wall corner to make it 2-1, a result that would see United earn a new League points total of fifty-two. With neither side showing a great deal of interest in the last 15 minutes of the game, the League season came to an end with a victory for the League champions.

The end of the game saw, what were for the time, some remarkable scenes. Around 1,000 fans congregated in front of the president's box for nearly an hour, insisting upon the various players appearing at the window. It was a fitting end to a great League season.

Elsewhere

Bolton's failure to go for a winner against Manchester United in their penultimate fixture had been made worse by them losing 1-0 at home to Notts County, who won in midweek at Chelsea and, as a consequence, stayed up at the Trotters' expense. Bolton joined Birmingham in Division Two. Bradford City and Leicester Fosse were promoted.

8

What was the Basis for United Winning the Title?

The first Manchester United side to win the First Division title did so by establishing a record points total for the time. This total would undoubtedly have been higher if the side had been able to maintain its first half of the season form when they literally swept all before them, losing just a single game, at Middlesbrough, from the first fourteen and then winning ten games in a row. This included one of the greatest performances ever by any Manchester United side when they thrashed the League champions Newcastle United 6-1 at St James' Park.

What undoubtedly held back Manchester United after the New Year was the need to change the first team. Whereas Ernest Mangnall needed to call on only fifteen players for the first half of the season, injuries and tiredness meant that twenty-three were to be used in the second. At the same time, there may also have been an element of complacency in the players' efforts when it became clear, after Newcastle had failed to revenge their earlier defeat in the return match at Bank Street in early February, that the title was as good as won and thoughts were turning towards the possibility of doing the League and FA Cup double.

That, of course, was to be foiled by a Fulham side that shocked the football world by beating the champions-elect in the quarter-finals in one of the greatest games ever played at Craven Cottage.

When the title was all but guaranteed at Everton on 8 April 1908, it followed a rousing last half hour of play by Ernest Mangnall's men. After playing the hosts off the park, they had been stunned when Everton levelled, but reacted by scoring almost immediately to restore the lead before winning 3-1 when Wall hit a last-minute goal. This was one of nineteen goals the outside-left contributed to the United championship success, just six fewer than Sandy Turnbull. It meant the pair contributed forty-four of the side's eighty-one League goals. Along with Billy Meredith, who continued to rip apart defences more than a decade and a half after he started playing professionally, Jimmy Bannister, who formed a deadly partnership with Meredith, and James Turnbull, with his boundless energy, dash and an eye for a goal, the had forged a deadly front five that tore the defence to shreds.

They were able to do so because of the formidable half-back line-up of Dick Duckworth, Alec Bell and Charlie Roberts. The latter, passing to all areas of the field, was unmatched by any player in the First Division in 1907/08. His heading, tackling and positional play was, to use a modern term, out of this world. Despite his delicate, youthful complexion, Roberts was an imposing figure who stood 6 feet tall and weighed over 13 stone. He was also extremely quick and had been timed at 11 seconds for 100 yards.

He was born on 6 April 1883 in Darlington, and left school at thirteen to become a furnace man in a nearby ironworks. In his six years there, he played for the works team and then joined Darlington St Augustine's, the top team in Darlington at the time. His presence in the team tightened up the defence considerably and led top amateur side Bishop Auckland, champions of the Northern League in 1900/01 and 1901/02, to seek his signature. Bishops later sent three of their own players – Warren Bradley, Bob Hardisty and Derek Lewin – to help out after the Munich tragedy in 1958. Bradley did so well, he later signed as a full-time professional at Old Trafford and added to his eleven amateur caps for England by playing three times for the professional side.

Roberts continued to demonstrate his talents and was selected to represent the Northern League against the Northern Alliance XI on 14 April 1903, where his performance attracted the attention of H. N. Nickson, manager of First Division Grimsby Town. A professional contract was signed ten days later, but the Mariners had suffered relegation and it meant Roberts' League debut on 1 September 1903 was a Division Two match at Blundell Park against Bradford City, who was also making its Football League debut. Over the following months, the new man's performances were so outstanding that many clubs began to consider signing him, including Manchester City, Derby County and Nottingham Forest. All three were First Division clubs.

On 22 April 1904, United chairman J. J. Bentley approached his Grimsby counterpart, Mr Bellows, in a London restaurant the day before the Cup final encounter between Manchester City and Bolton Wanderers. On the same day, Harry Stafford, the former Newton Heath captain who had persuaded J. H. Davies to save the club at the start of the century, and who now acted as chief fixer at the club, was in Grimsby talking directly to the Grimsby centre-half.

An impressed Roberts was prepared to forsake signing for a top-flight club and become a key player in a promotion bid at Bank Street. It seems unlikely he would have done so without at least some financial inducement being offered. Manchester City had just signed Glossop's Irvine Thornley the same month for a fee of over £500, and his father later reported that he himself had received half the fee. The FA banned him from pursuing a new career as an early football agent.

Stafford too was banned when the FA investigated affairs at Bank Street and announced on 13 December 1904, 'We find H. Stafford was cognisant of illegal payments having been made to players of Manchester United, and that proper accounts were not kept. For these reasons we recommend that H. Stafford should be suspended from football until 1 May 1907.' Stafford had clearly not acted alone, and his suspension ensured that club president J. J. Bentley – the Football League chairman, don't forget – avoided embarrassment and those with greater authority at Manchester United avoid their responsibilities.

Roberts made his debut for his new side on 23 April 1904, and was rated Man of the Match by the *Athletic News* in a 2-0 defeat of Burton United. The following season he was a member of a United rearguard that did not concede a goal in seven consecutive matches. The team also won a League record fourteen consecutive matches at one point and his form was so good that, despite being a Second Division player (only twice before had anyone from the Division been selected to play for England), he was selected to play for England in all three home international matches that season. England took the title with two wins and a draw.

Roberts missed the 0-0 draw against Barnsley when playing for England. He also missed the 2-0 defeat at Burnley on 11 March

1905, when he was among the scorers in a brilliant second-half comeback by the Football League in Glasgow, where the visitors recovered from being two down to win 3-2.

When United subsequently lost out to Bolton by three points for promotion, it was noted that victories at Barnsley and Bolton would have taken the club back into the top flight.

When England selectors, of which United chairman J. J. Bentley was one, became aware of United's concerns, Roberts was left out of the England side the following season. The problem for the Darlington lad was that he never got his place back after that. At least he was capped. Other Manchester United stars during this period, such as Moger, Duckworth, Burgess and Stacey, did not get a single cap between them. Despite capturing three of the eight trophies then up for grabs between 1907/08 and 1910/11, only Harold Halse and Wall were capped. This was at a time when almost fifty players appeared in England's nineteen international appearances.

With Roberts in the side, Manchester United won promotion in 1905/06. Then when Manchester United played the first game of the following season, it was Roberts who got them underway by scoring the first goal in the 2-1 victory over Bristol City, who had also been promoted and had equalled Manchester United's record of fourteen consecutive League victories during the 1905/06 season. Preston equalled the record in 1950/51. Roberts later scored a valuable header to ensure a draw with Manchester City in the first-ever top flight home derby.

Behind United's dazzling half-back line-up were full-backs with real quality in Dick Holden and George Burgess, initially, and later George Stacey. In goal, Harry Moger may never have been regarded highly enough by the England selectors to win an international cap, but he was an excellent 'keeper who was brave, fast off his line and punched well. In an age where 'keepers could take a real battering, he also gave as good as he got when facing opposing burly forwards.

Ernest Mangnall had fashioned a thrilling, winning side – one that can stand comparison to any Manchester United side that followed – and Meredith and Roberts would be strong contenders for inclusion in any all-time United XI.

9

WINNING THE CHARITY SHIELD IS INTERRUPTED BY THE FIRST OVERSEAS TOUR

As a result of winning the League, Manchester United was invited to play in the inaugural FA Charity Shield Match, which evolved from the Sheriff of London Charity Shield introduced at the end of the 1888/89 season as a professionals versus amateurs cup. However, when the latter fell out with the FA, a new format in which the Football League winners played the winners of the Southern League was devised and, as a result, United played QPR in a match held at Stamford Bridge. Dashing the FA's hopes that the new competition would be keenly anticipated, only 6,000 fans bothered to turn up on a day that saw the funeral of Prime Minister Campbell-Bannerman, who had died suddenly.

Monday 27 April 1908
FA Charity Shield   Stamford Bridge
Manchester United 1 (Meredith), QPR 1 (Cannon)
Manchester United: Moger, Stacey, Burgess, Duckworth, Roberts, Bell, Meredith, Bannister, J. Turnbull, A. Turnbull, Wall.
QPR: Shaw, MacDonald, Fidler, Lintott, J. McLean, Downing, Pentland, Cannon, Skilton, Gittons, Barnes.

This was certainly a game Manchester United should have won, as they were the better side throughout the 90 minutes. They did however fall behind when, early in the game, Frank Cannon scored for the West London side, but Meredith levelled the scores with a great goal when his shot from a tight angle completely beat Charlie Shaw in the QPR goal.

The Londoners were grateful to the 'keeper in the second period, however, when he saved Stacey's penalty. When the match ended it was agreed to be replayed at the start of the following season, as United was unavailable for the rest of the season with games still to play at Newcastle and Manchester before taking part in a tour of Austria and Hungary.

Evelyn Lintott

Lintott was QPR's first-ever England international, making his debut against Ireland in Belfast in a 3-1 win in February 1908. In total he was to make seven appearances for his country, for which he later gave his life when he was killed in action on the first day of the Somme, 1 July 1916.

Austro-Hungarian Tour, 1908

Following the season's end, the United board decided to reward the team with a trip to the Austro-Hungarian Empire. This took place only weeks before the England national team made their first-ever overseas tour to play four matches against Austria, Hungary and Bohemia (now part of the Czech Republic) – despite having won the League, no Manchester United players were picked to play.

After arriving in Paris on Saturday 2 May, United travelled to Zurich where, on 6 May, they played a combined Zurich XI, winning 4-2. On Saturday 9 May 1908, United beat SC Slavia 2-0 before a crowd of 5,000, with the goals coming from Picken and Bannister. On Sunday 10 May, United again beat SC Slavia 2-0 before a crowd of 10,000, who saw Picken and Bannister again score the goals. On Wednesday 13 May, United beat a Vienna XI side, consisting of players from Vienna SC, Vienna Athletic and Vienna FC, by four goals to nil in front of 2,000 people. The scorers were Turnbull with two, Picken and Wall. On Friday 15 May, United played Vienna Athletic, winning 5-0 with goals from Duckworth (2), Wall (2) and Turnbull.

The team then travelled by train to Budapest for two games. On 22 May, they beat Magyar Athletikai 6-2 after leading 4-1 at half-time. Scorers for Manchester United were Picken with three, Wall, Thomson and Duckworth. On Sunday 24 May, the final game of the tour, and the season, sparked a minor diplomatic incident. It finished Ferencváros Torna 0 Manchester United 7, with Bannister, Meredith (2), Wall (2), Picken and a penalty from goalkeeper Moger completing the rout. There seems to be some uncertainty as to what exactly the cause was, but there was no doubt that abuse, and more worryingly stones, some of considerable size, were thrown at the players. As a consequence, a number were injured, although none seriously.

On 26 May, the *Manchester Guardian*, carrying an article from Reuters in Budapest, reported on 'the inability of the onlookers to appreciate differences between the rules obtaining in England and those which are recognized here'.

It was reported that the referee had wanted to send off three of the United side. There had been arguments over the use of goal judges stationed on the goal line, and even more so when they appeared to be shouting out to the referee what decisions to make. Thomson appears to have grabbed hold of the referee, which the Reuters news agency, making the following comment, reported as an attempt to 'explain matters':

> In the discussion one or two of the visitors placed their hands persuasively on the referee's shoulder and the spectators in the cheap seats, misinterpreting the action, thought the Manchester men were trying to attack him. Considerable excitement resulted.

Follow-up reports in the paper, and in the *Manchester Courier*, do not suggest that at this point stones were thrown. Instead, they suggest in fact that when apologies were offered, the match was restarted with all twenty-two players on the pitch.

However, after the match had finished, some of the crowd, who were believed to have bet heavily on their side beating Manchester United, began throwing stones at the away players. At this point, a body of mounted policemen came to their rescue and, with swords drawn, escorted them from the ground. After taking the players to what was felt to be a safe distance, the police then dispersed and more stones were thrown.

When peace was finally restored, it was possible for both teams to attend the after-match dinner. The United side was also accompanied to the station by their hosts, and it was reported that the First Division champions had agreed to play in Budapest the following year after the hosts offered their sincere apologies for the unfortunate events.

Whether this was really the intention we will never know. But by Friday morning (29 May 1908), when the side arrived back in London – but not until they had played a final game on 25 May against a mixed team drawn from Vienna clubs that was won 3-2 – Ernest Mangnall had announced that they would not be playing Budapest or Slavia again. In addition, the United boss was reported in the *Manchester Courier* as saying that 'the idea of the foreign players seemed to be that all they do is to kick, push and hack. They go for the men and not the ball.' He finished by complaining about the standard of the refereeing.

When the side finally arrived back in Manchester, where Mangnall again described the tour as 'a big success, except for Budapest and Slavia', they were met with what the *Courier* described as 'a hearty welcome from a number of friends and supporters'.

Saturday 29 August 1908

FA Charity Shield Replay   Stamford Bridge
Manchester United 4 (Turnbull 3, Wall), QPR 0
Manchester United: Moger, Stacey, Burgess, Duckworth, Roberts, Bell, Meredith, Bannister, J. Turnbull, Picken, Wall.
QPR: Shaw, MacDonald, Fidler, Lintot, J. McLean, Downing, McNaught, Cannon, Skilton, Gittons, Barnes .

In a match held over from the previous season, Manchester United returned to the form they had exhibited in the first half, and QPR were fortunate not to suffer an embarrassing defeat. Special permission had to be given for the game to take place before the official starting date of the season, which was then 1 September, and a good number of newspapers were of the opinion that it should have been denied.

The newspapers were also critical of the decision of QPR not to play Fred Pentland, who they had transferred to Middlesbrough during the summer, the feeling being that he should not have missed out playing in this most prestigious of events due to circumstances over which he had no control. Pentland travelled to the game and won the approval of FA secretary Frederick Wall to play, but his former club refused him a place in the side. Pentland later managed

Atlético Madrid and Athletic Bilbao, taking the latter to two league titles and five Spanish Cups during the club's most successful period ever. Pentland still remains revered by the Basque supporters. His place in the replayed 1908 Charity Shield match was taken by John McNaught, and his teammates, showing solidarity with Pentland, refused to pass the ball to him.

From the start, Charlie Shaw was the busier of the two 'keepers, punching clear a series of crosses before tipping over a beauty from Bannister. Picken was then denied by a last gasp John MacDonald tackle, but on 25 minutes Meredith got past Sam Downing and his cross was turned home by James Turnbull to the cheers of the crowd, who clearly appreciated the style and panache of a United side in full flow. Ernest Mangnall's men were showing some superb skills, with immaculate passing between the half-backs and forwards tearing QPR apart. Turnbull then doubled the northern side's advantage.

Perhaps certain of their victory, Manchester United then relaxed and might have paid for their complacency, but Alfred Gittens was unable to get round Stacey before Frank Cannon's shot was easily saved by Moger, back in the United goal after missing the original match in April.

On 56 minutes, Wall made it 3-0 and just before the end of the game, Turnbull completed his hat-trick to round off a thoroughly convincing 4-0 victory that ensured Manchester United added another new trophy, the Charity Shield, to the Football League one they had captured for the first time at the end of the previous season. All they now had to do was win the FA Cup in 1909.

Statistics – League and FA Cup Matches Only

Results
Aston Villa [A] 4-1: Meredith 2, Bannister, Wall
Liverpool [H] 4-0: Sandy Turnbull 3, Wall
Middlesbrough [H] 2-1: Sandy Turnbull 2
Middlesbrough [A] 1-2: Bannister
Sheffield United [H] 2-1: Sandy Turnbull 2
Manchester City [A] Lancashire Senior Cup 3-0: Sandy Turnbull, James Turnbull, Wall
Chelsea [A] 4-1: Meredith 2, Sandy Turnbull, Bannister

Nottingham Forest [H] 4-0: Bannister, James Turnbull, Wall, o.g.
Newcastle United [A] 6-1: Wall 2, Meredith, J. Turnbull, S. Turnbull,
  Roberts
Bolton [H] Lancashire Senior Cup 2-0: J. Turnbull, S. Turnbull
Blackburn Rovers [A] 5-1: S. Turnbull 3, J. Turnbull 2
Bolton Wanderers [H] 2-1: S. Turnbull, J. Turnbull
Oldham Athletic [N] Lancashire Senior Cup semi-final 1-3: S. Turnbull
Birmingham [A] 4-3: Meredith 2, J. Turnbull, Wall
Everton [H] 4-3: Wall 2, Meredith, Roberts
Sunderland [A] 2-1: S. Turnbull 2
Woolwich Arsenal 4-2: S. Turnbull 4
The Wednesday 0-2
Bristol City [H] 2-1: Wall 2
Notts County [A] 1-1: Meredith
Manchester City [A] 3-1: S. Turnbull 2, Wall
Bury [H] 2-1: J. Turnbull, Meredith
PNE [A] 0-0
Bury [A] 1-0: Wall
Blackpool [H] FA Cup 3-1: Meredith, Wall 2
Sheffield United [A] 0-2
Chelsea [H] 1-0: J. Turnbull
Chelsea [H] FA Cup 1-0: S. Turnbull
Newcastle United [H] 1-1: J. Turnbull
Blackburn Rovers [H] 1-2: S. Turnbull [pen.]
Aston Villa [A] FA Cup 2-0: S. Turnbull, Wall
Birmingham [H] 1-0: S. Turnbull
Fulham [A] FA Cup 1-2: J. Turnbull
Sunderland [H] 3-0: Bell, Berry, o.g.
Manchester City [H] Manchester Cup 1-0: Wall [pen.]
Woolwich Arsenal [A] 0-1
Liverpool [A] 4-7: Wall 2, J. Turnbull, Bannister
The Wednesday [H] 4-1: Wall 2, Halse, S. Turnbull
Bristol City [A] 1-1: Wall
Everton [A] 3-1: Halse, Wall, S. Turnbull
Notts County [H] 0-1
Stockport County [N] Manchester Cup Semi-Final 3-1: Halse 3
Nottingham Forest [A] 0-2
Manchester City [A] 0-0
Aston Villa [H] 1-2: Picken
Bolton Wanderers [A] 2-2: Halse, Stacey

PNE [H] 2-1: o.g., Halse
QPR [N] Charity Shield 1-1: Meredith
Bury [N] Manchester Cup final 1-0: Bannister
QPR [N] Charity Shield Replay 4-0: Turnbull 3, Wall

League Goal scorers (81)

Sandy Turnbull	25
George Wall	18
James Turnbull	10
Billy Meredith	10
Harold Halse	4
James Bannister	5
Own Goals	3
Charlie Roberts	2
Picken, Berry, Stacey, Bell	1 each

Final League Table

	Games Played	Points	
Manchester United	38	52	(23-6-9, 81-48)
Aston Villa	38	43	
Manchester City	38	43	
Newcastle United	38	42	
The Wednesday	38	42	
Middlesbrough	38	41	
Bury	38	39	
Liverpool	38	38	
Bristol City	38	36	
Everton	38	36	
PNE	38	36	
Chelsea	38	36	
Blackburn Rovers	38	36	
Woolwich Arsenal	38	36	
Sunderland	38	35	
Sheffield United	38	35	
Notts County	38	34	
Bolton	38	33	
Birmingham	38	30	

League Appearances

Meredith	37
Bannister	36
Wall	36
Duckworth	36
Bell	35
Roberts	32
Sandy Turnbull	29
Moger	29
Burgess	27
Holden	26
James Turnbull	26
Stacey	18
Broomfield	9
Picken	9
Menzies	6
Halse	6
Downie	5
Thomson	3
Berry	3
Hulme	1
Wilson	1
Whiteside	1
McGillvray	1
Dalton	1
Williams	1

10

SPIRITED START TO
A NEW SEASON

When Manchester United began the defence of their Premier League title in 2013/14, the press coverage in the week leading up to the opening game of the season away to Swansea was immense. There was much less coverage when Ernest Mangnall's side began the 1908/09 season. This started officially on a Tuesday, but, having been allowed to play in the Charity Shield against QPR three days earlier, the champions did not play on 1 September 1908.

Manchester United's first League game of the season was away to Preston North End on Saturday 5 September 1908. The *Daily Mirror* made no mention of the game on the Friday and had the briefest of reviews on the match day itself:

> Manchester United, who made such hacks of Queen's Park Rangers last Saturday at Stamford Bridge, go to Preston. Here they meet a much better side – both Preston (who drew 0-0 with Chelsea on the opening day of the season) and the Rangers have appeared at Stamford Bridge, so it is possible to judge – but it will be a great team that stops the United in the opening months of this season, and I do not think that Preston will start the stopping.

It is perhaps also worth noting that, while the coverage was sparse, even back in 1908, Manchester United were known as just United.

On Monday 7 September 1908, the *Daily Mirror* had this to say about Manchester United winning 3-0 at Preston: 'Manchester United put on another great victory at Preston.'

With Sandy Turnbull out injured, Picken retained his place at inside-left, and with the exception of James Turnbull, who replaced Bannister in the starting line-up, the Manchester United side that played at Deepdale was the same as the one that had played against Preston when the sides met on the final day of the 1907/08 League season.

Halse had scored in the 2-1 victory at Bank Street in April 1908, and he was also on the scoresheet in a much easier victory just over four months later, when another two from Jimmy Turnbull helped the away side to a 3-0 victory.

Two days later, Turnbull repeated his exploits as Bury was beaten 2-1 at Bank Street. Two victories quickly became three when, in a remarkable match, Middlesbrough were beaten 6-3 at Bank Street. Steve Bloomer scored twice for the Teessiders, but he was outshone by Turnbull, who scored four times. The 25,000-strong crowd were left thrilled by the United performance, with many leaving already convinced their favourites were en route to retaining their title. The handsome victory against a side that had finished in sixth place in 1907/08 was even more remarkable as the home side lost Burgess to injury after just 15 minutes. Mangnall had chosen to swap Halse from inside-right to inside-left, and his partnership with Wall had proved more productive than the Meredith-Halse one in the first two matches of the season. Turnbull's pace and powerful shooting had kept Tim Williamson at full stretch for the entire 90 minutes.

There then followed a fourth consecutive victory when City were overcome 2-1 at Hyde Street, where Halse was joined on the scoresheet by the prolific Turnbull, who now had nine in four matches. The game marked the first-team debut of Harold Hardman who, as an amateur, had been able to transfer from Everton to Manchester United at the start of the season. Hardman was a remarkable man who coped with the pace of the professional game even though he remained a full-time solicitor throughout his thirteen-year football career, during which he made two FA Cup final appearances – winning one and losing one – and also played four times for England. He arrived in Manchester in the months leading up to the Olympic Games, where he won a gold medal as a member of the England football team that beat Denmark 2-0 in final of the competition held at the White City, London.

Although Hardman only found time to play four first team matches for Manchester United, he proved highly influential at the club. He went on to serve for over half a century as a director, including fourteen years as chairman.

Manchester United won their fifth League match in a row on 26 September 1908 when they beat Liverpool 3-2. A large away following had been encouraged by a bright opening from their side, and Charlie Roberts was forced to clear hastily on a number of occasions. When the home side did finally manage to get forward, they scored on their first attack when Turnbull headed down Meredith's cross for Halse to finish. Sam Hardy in the Liverpool goal is arguably the club's finest-ever 'keeper, but his mistake then allowed Halse to double his tally and make it 2-0. When Jack Cox made it 2-1 on 54 minutes, the home side restored their two-goal lead when Hardy couldn't hold on to a Wall blockbuster and Turnbull made it 3-1. The Liverpool 'keeper then made two fabulous saves from Wall and Meredith to partly atone for his earlier mistakes before Alex Raisbeck scored from the spot after Stacey handled.

In the search for an equaliser, the away side was guilty of giving away too many fouls and when the final whistle sounded, the victors had gone to the top of the table after news came through that leaders Newcastle United had lost.

In the sixth League game of 1908/09, Manchester United were held 2-2 by Bury, whose goals were scored by Hibbert. Sandy Turnbull returned for the first time in the season, and Halse and Wall scored for the champions. A week later, a 2-1 success at home to Sheffield United, in which Bell scored twice, made it thirteen points from fourteen. The away side may well have grabbed a deserved point if Ernest Needham had not been forced to leave proceedings early due to an injury. Despite being in the twilight of his career, the England international remained an influential figure on the pitch.

United's luck did not hold out in the eighth League game of the season, when a dashing Aston Villa side thrilled its fans by beating the visitors 3-1. Amid great enthusiasm, George Reeves and then Hampton beat Moger to make it 2-0 at the interval. Reeves made it 3-0 after a dribble past the United defence was followed by a fine finish. Although Halse reduced the arrears, the pressure exerted on the Villa goal failed to alter the score line on a day after the flying trials conducted by the British Army were partially successful: the airplane being tested flew for a short distance before crash landing. In the meantime, Mr Will Thorne MP appeared at Bow Street court after being summoned for his speech to the unemployed in Trafalgar Square the previous Saturday, when he had urged anyone who was hungry to 'rush every baker's shop in London'.

Having drawn with Nottingham Forest 2-2 at Bank Street, the champions made the long journey to face Sunderland at Roker Park. Things started to go wrong when Burgess was carried off with a twisted knee, and when Downie met the same fate it left the away side with just nine players for the final 50 minutes of the match. The 6-1 defeat in which Arthur Brown, George Holley and Arthur Bridgett all scored twice was, at the time, United's record defeat in the top flight – Liverpool having beaten United 7-1 in a Second Division fixture in 1895/96. Duckworth in the United defence was outstanding and helped keep the score down with a series of well-timed tackles.

A second consecutive defeat, this time at home to Chelsea the following weekend by 1-0, saw the defeated side drop down the table to sixth, six points behind leaders Everton. To make matters worse, Sandy Turnbull had been carried off the pitch and would not return until Christmas.

However, Mangnall's side then picked themselves up to win five of the next six matches. Having overcome Blackburn Rovers 3-1 at Ewood Park, they faced Bradford City for the first time ever, and won fairly comfortably by two goals to nil. The game was Duckworth's benefit match and with only 14,000 present, he was grateful he had already been guaranteed £500 beforehand by his employers. The United half-back was wildly cheered by those who were at the match and again performed with distinction.

A 3-1 home success against Sheffield Wednesday then put United within three points of leaders Everton with a match in hand. The following weekend, the two sides faced each other at Goodison Park.

The game was a benefit match for two of Everton's most faithful players – Harry Makepeace and Robert Balmer, who both played in the 1906 and 1907 FA Cup finals. The large crowd meant receipts were upwards of £1,000, and afterwards both men received a cheque for £500 10s 6d at a special dinner arranged on their behalf, which was attended by all the home players and the Everton officials.

This sum would have been sufficient to allow Makepeace and Balmer to buy an average house at around £200 and still have the deposit for a car costing £400. Owning one would have made you part of a select elite, as only 50,000 individuals did so in 1908. There were, however, moves to considerably expand ownership levels and in 1912, the Model T Ford was rolling off production lines at the company's new factory in Trafford Park. Petrol cost around 5d a litre in 1909.

The game had a sensational opening when the returning Hardman raced beyond Irish international Valentine Harris. When he dropped his cross into the box, Halse nudged aside John McConnachie to drive his side ahead. The United side was missing both Turnbulls, and with Meredith playing at half-back, the forward line was as follows: Hardman, Livingstone, Halse, Bannister and Wall.

With the crowd behind them, the League leaders levelled when Jack Sharp – who represented England internationally at cricket and football – drilled a fine ball for Bert Freeman to race away and beat Moger. The home side took the lead early in the second half when George Barlow's shot was too hot for the United 'keeper, and when the ball ran loose the attacker forced home the rebound. The away side was quickly level when Bannister beat Irish international Billy Scott, brother of Liverpool 'keeper Elisha, with a powerful shot.

The winning goal was a fine effort by Freeman. It was one of his thirty-eight League goals during the season and made him the first Everton player to score more than thirty League goals during a season. His total was to make him easily the highest scorer in Division One in 1908/09, with his nearest challenger, Hibbert at Bury, scoring twelve fewer. Freeman's scoring helped him win his first cap in March 1909, and he scored in a 2-0 win over Wales at Nottingham. Freeman later joined Burnley and he scored the winning goal in the 1914 FA Cup final, when the East Lancs side beat Liverpool 1-0.

Everton's victory extended their lead over second placed Newcastle United who, that same afternoon, suffered a 9-1 home defeat to local rivals Sunderland, a result that remains the joint highest away victory in top flight football in England.

Back at home the following weekend, Manchester United was watched by a crowd of 10,000, who saw Wall notch a hat-trick that, added to a single effort from Picken, was enough to overcome Leicester Fosse 4-2. A single goal by Halse on 19 December 1908 was sufficient to ensure two points in a 1-0 victory away to Woolwich Arsenal, but playing on Christmas Day there was a 2-1 reverse at St James' Park. The return 24 hours later on Boxing Day saw the home side gain revenge over the Magpies when a single goal by Halse was sufficient to ensure both points for the home side. With Sandy Turnbull returning to the line-up, there was a seven-goal thriller on New Year's Day, and his goal, along with a Roberts' effort and two from Halse, saw Notts County beaten 4-3 at Bank Street. The result left the victors in third place just two points behind leaders Everton with a game in hand.

OPPOSITE THIS PLAQUE WAS THE
BANK STREET GROUND
HOME OF
MANCHESTER UNITED
FORMERLY NEWTON HEATH F.C.
1893 TO 1910

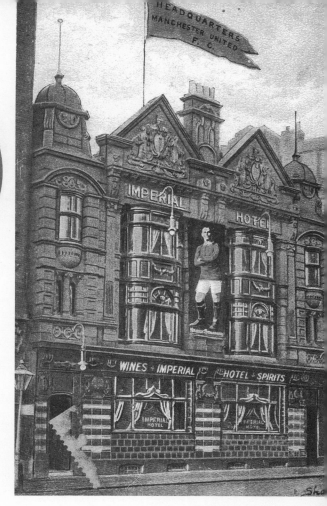

Above: 1. A red plaque less than a mile from Etihad Stadium is all that remains of Manchester United's stay at Bank Street, before their move to Old Trafford in 1910.

Right: 2. Manchester United Football Club headquarters.

Below: 3. This picture of Charlie Sagar scoring against Bristol City in 1905 gives some example of Bank Street in all its glory.

Left: 4. George Stacey.

Above: 5. Enoch West topped the First Division scoring charts with Nottingham Forest in 1907/08 and signed for Manchester United in 1910.

Below: 6. J. J. Bentley.

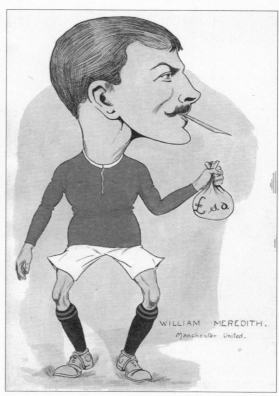

WILLIAM MEREDITH.
Manchester United.

Above: 7. Alex Young of Everton.

Right: 8. Billy Meredith.

Below: 9. Charlie Roberts.

Left: 10. Play-up Newton Heath postcard, forerunners to Manchester United between 1878 and 1902.

Above: 11. Bert Freeman of Everton topped the First Division scoring charts with thirty-eight League goals in 1908/09.

Below: 12. Middle pages of the 1909 Cup final programme, a copy of which sold for a world-record price of £23,500 in 2012.

Captions

Football Wizard

Above: 13. Harold Makepeace of Everton is unique in the world of sport by winning an FA Cup, League Championship and County Cricket Championship medal as well as representing England internationally at football and cricket.

Right: 14. Machester United, League champions 1908.

Below: 15. The League-winning side with their trophy.

MANCHESTER UNITED FOOTBALL CLUB, 1908-9.

Club Colours : Red and White.

BOYS FRIEND FOOTBALL SUPPLEMENT

[Photo by Chambers & Co., Clapton.]

PLAYERS, OFFICIALS AND TROPHIES.

DOWNIE.   BURGESS.
NUTTALL   H. STAFFORD   BROOMFIELD   STACEY   DUCKWORTH   HOLDEN   BELL   MOGER   BACON
(Director).
H. TAYLOR   PICKEN   BANNISTER   J. TURNBULL   ROBERTS   HALSE   A. TURNBULL   J. E. MANGNALL
(Director).   (Secretary).
MEREDITH   WALL
Association Charity Shield.   League Cup.   Manchester Cup.

Above: 16. Newcastle United's Albert Shepherd was the top scorer in Division One in 1910/11 with twenty-five League goals. Shepherd also finished as top scorer in the League with Bolton in 1905/06. He is seen here scoring for Newcastle at Roker Park.

Below left: 17. Ernest Needham of Sheffield United was one of the finest footballers of his generation.

Below right: 18. George Holley of Sunderland.

Above: 19. George Elliott of Middlesbrough.

Right: 20. 1908 Charity Shield, Manchester United beat Queens Park Rangers to claim the shield.

Below: 21. Winning Charity Shield team.

"FOR THE BEST CAUSE OF ALL."

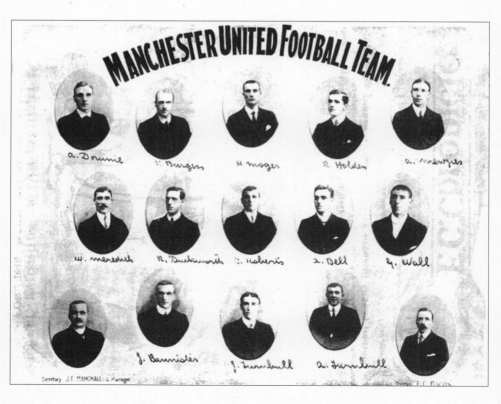

22. The Rocca Brigade were a gaudily dressed, boisterous group of Manchester fans who took their name from Louis Rocca, the son of a prominent local Italian ice cream businessman.

23. The famous Outcasts picture. Back row, from left to right: J. Picken, W. Corbett, R. Holden, H. Burgess, J. Clough, B. Meredith, G. Boswell (Players' Union assistant secretary). Front row: G. Wall, A. Turnbull, C. Roberts, T. Coleman, R. Duckworth. All the players were with Manchester United except Everton's Coleman.

Parkinson chalked another couple on the slate.

Above: 24. Jack Parkinson scored his eighth and ninth goals of the 1909/10 season as Liverpool beat Manchester United 3-2 in October 1909. Parkinson was to finish as top scorer in Division One at the end of the season with thirty goals.

Below: 25. The 1909 FA Cup final was played at the Crystal Palace in South London.

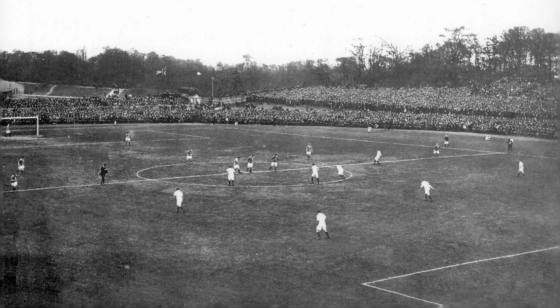

26. The 1910 English squad before their tour to South Africa. The squad included three Manchester United players – George Wall, Dick Duckworth and Vince Hayes.

27. Manchester United *v.* Sunderland programme for the final game of the 1910/11 season. Although the players are numbered in the programme, they did not have numbers on their shirts.

The football season opened yesterday with every prospect of the dispute being finally settled.

Above: 28. A last-minute agreement prevented a strike by Manchester United players on the opening day of the 1909/10 season.

Below: 29. The FA Cup semi-final replay between Everton and Barnsley on 31 March 1910 was the first occasion when Old Trafford hosted a prestigious match involving sides other than Manchester United. Second Division Barnsley won the match 3-0.

30. The 1909 FA Cup final.

31. Sandy Turnbull scores the winning goal in the 1909 FA Cup final.

32. Action at the first United *v.* City derby match to be played at Old Trafford in September 1910. The home side won 2-1.

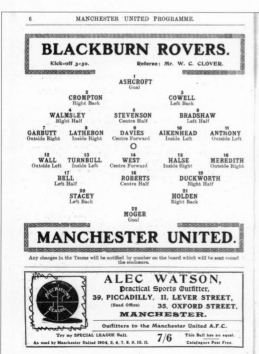

33. Manchester United *v.* Blackburn Rovers programme, 1910.

THE LAST VISITOR !

[By kind permission of the *Birmingham Sporting Mail*.]

The Aston Lion: If there are any more lion-hunters about, just tell 'em I'm not at home.

[The Villa wound up their home engagements in the League last Saturday by defeating Manchester United.]

Above: 34. Manchester United team photograph, 1910/11.
Note the 'keepers wearing their caps, with Moger in the middle row easily the tallest player in the squad.

Left: 35. A cartoon from the Aston Villa newspaper pokes fun at Manchester United after their side beat the Lancastrians 4-2 toward the end of the season. The conquered side recovered to snatch the title from the Birmingham side.

Championship Hopes Fade as FA Cup Gets Underway

Two defeats, at Preston by 2-0 and a hammering by five goals at Middlesbrough, were a big blow. Alf Common scored twice for Boro. He was signed from Sunderland in 1905 at a cost of £1,000, a fee considered so enormous that many predicted it marked the end of football. Middlesbrough's move was designed to avoid relegation and this brought its own condemnation because, while it was considered acceptable to purchase players to win titles, it was considered immoral to do so to avoid the drop. The *Athletic News* commented that, 'As a matter of commerce, ten young recruits at £100 apiece might have paid better, and as a matter of sport, the Second Division would be more honourable than retention of place by purchase.' Common's arrival helped prevent Boro going down.

Always anxious about rising transfer fees, the FA even went as far as introducing a £350 limitation fee on 1 January 1908. That was expunged at the FA annual meeting four months later, and transfer fees have continued to increase ever since.

With Halse out injured, Bill Berry, who was originally signed as a stop-gap measure as United awaited the arrival of Meredith from City in 1906/07, was asked to play centre-forward. The Sunderland-born player struggled – the game at Ayresome Park proved his last for Manchester United and he was sold soon afterwards to Second Division Stockport County.

On 16 January 1909, the first round of the FA Cup kicked off, with United facing Southern League side Brighton at Bank Street. The poor results in the previous game, plus bad weather, combined to reduce the crowd to just 8,300. As a result, both clubs received less than £100 in receipts for their efforts (the total gate receipt was £238). Of those present at the game, 270 had journeyed by midnight excursion from Brighton, arriving at 6.45 a.m. Among the trippers was Captain A. B. S. Fraser, the mayor of Brighton, whose late uncle was Bishop Fraser, a statue of whom still stands in Albert Square today.

The Brighton side were heartily cheered on to the field by their small band of fans. At right-back was Joseph Leeming who, prior to moving south, had represented Bury in a number of different positions over many years. He hailed from the old Association stronghold, Turton, and played 280 times for Bury and more than 200 times for Brighton. Leeming twice won the FA Cup with Bury, first when Southampton were beaten 4-0 in the 1900 final and then in 1903, when Derby were thrashed 6-0 in the final with Leeming scoring twice. Back in Manchester, Leeming had a fine game.

The home side had both Turnbulls in it for the first time in over two months and yet still failed to sparkle. The heavy pitch, almost devoid of grass and with a smattering of snow on it, proved a handicap for the players and several sustained injuries, including Bell, James Turnbull and Brighton left-back Stewart. All three had to leave the field of play.

Also leaving the arena was Meredith, whose dismissal with 5 minutes remaining left his side with just eight players. The *Manchester Courier* was sympathetic to the Welshman's plight – Meredith was unwilling to go and several of the Brighton players supported his appeals for clemency – and felt that if it was true and he had kneed his opponent, then the offence was not worthy of being dismissed. The paper criticised the referee for having failed to take greater control of the game and bemoaned that he had sent the United winger off for the first time in his career. The dismissal was to see Meredith suspended for the subsequent Cup matches with Blackburn Rovers and Everton.

The Man of the Match was the Brighton 'keeper Bob Whiting, who made many fine saves and maintained the reputation earned from his two previous seasons at Chelsea. Because of his long goal kicks, Whiting was nicknamed 'Pom Pom' in reference to a powerful automatic, long-distance gun deployed by the British Army at the time.

Whiting was to serve with the Footballers' Battalion during the First World War and lost his life on 28 April 1917 when he was killed by shellfire while attending his wounded colleagues during a military action near Vimy Ridge. Although this news was bad enough for his widow Nellie, it was made worse for some considerable time afterwards by the allegation that he had been shot for desertion, a claim that was without foundation.

Moger in the United goal, meanwhile, had very little to do, although the former Blackburn Rovers forward Martin did miss an easy chance and late in the game Robertson's header flicked the bar en route into the drenched crowd behind the goal.

The only goal of the game came after 23 minutes, when a poor clearance on a pitch that was now little more than a mud bath in parts let in Halse and he beat the Brighton 'keeper with a cross ground shot.

Whiting kept his side in the game with two tremendous saves from Roberts and Wall early in the second half, and this provided an opportunity for a late surge by the visitors in search of an equaliser. The *Brighton Argus* felt that withstanding the pressure had not been undertaken especially sportingly as, in addition to supporting the referee's decision to dismiss Meredith, the paper's reporter criticised the challenge made by Sandy Turnbull that led to Stewart leaving the field as well as a 'strong challenge' on Longstaff in the last minute of the game. According to the *Argus*, the 'shoddy tactics adopted by United in the second half came in for much adverse criticism, even from their own followers'.

The only goal of the game came from Sandy Turnbull, and it was one of 101 goals he scored during his time at Manchester United.

The miner's son from Scotland became a coal miner at fourteen and, after his father died, the main breadwinner in a family of seven children. He continued to play for local side, Hurlford Thistle, and his form was good enough to earn him a professional contract at Manchester City. His big shoulders, quick feet and active brain were combined with a rugged determination and a sharp, acute shot. His indiscretion in becoming the first United player sent off in a Manchester derby match in December 1907 was not the only time he got into trouble in the first decade of the twentieth century, and the United board minutes for the 1900s record him as being 'insubordinate to directors' on a number of occasions.

Turnbull played in the derby game that followed the Cup match with Brighton, but the star was new signing George Livingstone. The Scottish international had played in the same Manchester City side as Meredith, Burgess and Turnbull that had won the FA Cup in 1904. Following the ban for illegal payments in 1906, Livingstone was sold to Rangers before returning to Manchester in January 1909. His arrival saw him pair up with Meredith on the right and allow Halse to move to centre-forward against City. His two goals on his debut, combined with an effort from Wall, resulted in a 3-1 victory for United.

The following weekend saw the short trip to Anfield. A victory for fourth-placed United was vital to keep within touching distance of new leaders Newcastle United. The away side started brightly, and it was no surprise when Turnbull headed home following some fine play by Livingstone and Wall. Hardy then made two fabulous saves from Meredith before the Liverpool 'keeper was fortunate when Duckworth's shot crashed back into play off the crossbar. Having outplayed their hosts, the away side left the pitch at half-time just a goal ahead. The failure to take their chances cost them dearly when Arthur Goddard, Tom Chorlton and Joe Hewitt netted to give Liverpool a 3-1 victory.

The defeated side faced Everton on 6 February 1909 in the second round of the FA Cup. With Meredith suspended, Halse was moved to outside-right when both Turnbulls were passed fit to play and Livingstone retained his place in the side. A crowd of 35,217 was boosted by a large following from Liverpool. Their side suffered a first away defeat of the season the following Saturday when they had lost 4-0 at Manchester City.

The game proved to be a very tight affair in which the home side was forced to defend deeply in the early stages of the match. The Everton attackers though were occasionally guilty of taking too long to shoot, and they were foiled by a United rearguard that worked heroically to deny them any clear goal-scoring opportunities.

The game was decided by a single goal. Was it a fluke or a brilliant one? It came just before the interval when Halse showed great agility – and presence of mind – when a half-clearance by the Everton defence saw the ball bound loose and the United attacker meet it with a flying kick, sending it flashing into the net.

Having taken the lead, United stepped up their efforts to deny the away side any opportunities of getting back into the match. Strong challenges were made on both sides and the large crowd roared its approval. In the second half, Roberts was seen rallying his men and his fine passing out to both wings had the Everton backs in constant trouble. The United captain was the Man of the Match and the *Liverpool Courier* of 8 February reported that, 'At half-back Roberts was the centre of attraction, and in the disposition of his side when danger threatened he displayed characteristic judgment.' United progressed by the narrowest of margins.

The following weekend, Manchester United grabbed a 0-0 draw at Bramall Lane in the League before returning to Bank Street to face Blackburn Rovers in the next round of the FA Cup.

Such was the away side's record of five successes in the FA Cup that for Rovers fans, the cup had become almost a 'holy grail', with the League seen as inferior. Among the crowd of 38,500, there was a substantial away following, many of who still managed a great night out in Manchester afterwards, even after seeing their side heavily beaten 6-1.

If the margin of victory was harsh, it was nevertheless a reward for a fine exhibition of attacking play by the home side, who saw both Turnbulls score three times. For once, England's finest full-back, Crompton, was given the run around out on the United left where Sandy Turnbull and Wall ran him ragged. The first goal saw Wall draw the Rovers man towards him before delivering an exquisite pass to his partner, who finished with a beautiful shot beyond Jimmy Ashcroft, signed from Arsenal at the start of the season, in the away goal.

Having swiftly added to their advantage with two further goals, the home side were briefly pegged back when William 'Tinker' Davies, a colleague in the Welsh side with Meredith, reduced the arrears. Thereafter, for a good 15 minutes, the work of Moger in goal was superb, and he saved many good shots before the United half-back line hit back with some great passing to allow the home forwards to finish off the tie.

Despite having won 6-1, the *Manchester Courier* report on Monday 22 February 1909 noted that Halse and Livingstone had rarely got the better of tough-tackling Arthur Cowell and Billy Bradshaw, a tripe dresser until he became a professional footballer, on the Rovers left. The paper concluded, 'it is evident that Livingstone is seen to better advantage with Meredith by his side'. Victory put Ernest Mangnall's side within two matches of the FA Cup final, a competition that no United side had won in the past.

Off the pitch meanwhile, on 26 February 1909, the general public saw Kinemacolor, the first film shown in colour, at the

Palace Theatre in London. It was invented by George Albert Smith of Brighton. Cinema, in conjunction with sport, subsequently revolutionised the world through developing mass culture for the modern urban society.

Back in the League in 1909, a disappointing performance away to Nottingham Forest and 2-0 defeat meant United was ten points behind leaders Newcastle United with just sixteen matches remaining. It was clear that, barring a minor miracle, the League trophy was not going to be retained, and so attention naturally centred on capturing the FA Cup. In fact, the side led by Charlie Roberts was to win just one League game in the remaining matches and finished well down in thirteenth place with thirty-seven points, just three more than relegated City, whose fans must have looked on enviously as their local rivals moved towards equalling their 1904 FA Cup exploits.

12

FA Cup Progress

In the quarter-finals of the competition, United played Second Division Burnley at Turf Moor. The Clarets were captained by former Villa man Leake, and he lined up against the returning Meredith in a game that had captured the imagination of the local public.

There is a saying that every side that wins the cup enjoys a touch of luck along the way. Such was the case for Manchester United at Burnley in 1909.

The match at Burnley meant a return to his former ground for Ernest Mangnall, who in 1899 had replaced Harry Bradshaw as secretary/manager at Turf Moor. It did not prove a particularly successful appointment as Burnley was relegated from the First Division at the end of Mangnall's first season and at the end of the 1902/03 season, the team was bottom of the Second Division and had to apply for re-election. Mangnall left for Bank Street shortly after. He was replaced at Turf Moor by Spen Whittaker, who improved Burnley's fortune but tragically died when he fell from his car in April 1910. A benefit match was played at Turf Moor against Manchester United with the proceeds going to his family.

Burnley had beaten Bristol Rovers, Crystal Palace and Spurs in the earlier rounds, and the tie was the first time they had been drawn at home in the tournament that season. On the morning of the game with United, the *Daily Mirror* commented, 'Burnley play a rough, fierce game, which tells in the Cup-ties, and roughness is not always the limit of their forcefulness.' The paper's reporter was clearly looking forward to the contest and the speedy Burnley forwards. He commented that Manchester would have 'their work cut out this afternoon', and '[would] do well to draw.'

That certainly proved the case and the League champions were fortunate when, with just 17 minutes remaining, a snow blizzard forced the abandonment of the game when they were losing 1-0.

The bitter conditions meant that an expected record crowd to beat the 24,000 that had watched the replayed game with Spurs was not achieved. Special excursion trains from surrounding towns were not as filled as was hoped prior to kick off at 3.30 p.m., and those paying for admission totalled 15,421. Leake was able to win the toss for the home side and as expected chose to play with the wind and snow at his back.

The game started with the home side searching for an early goal. Forty-five years later when these same sides met in the FA Cup third round, there was a sensational start when Burnley scored twice in the first 60 seconds and, after 5 minutes of the game, it was 2-2. Burnley went on to win 5-3.

In 1909, Burnley quickly exploited the conditions much better than their illustrious opponents, with the half-backs getting the ball out wide to their wingers at every opportunity.

With the United defenders struggling to keep their feet, a host of chances were made in the first period, and a half-time lead by just one goal was the least that Burnley deserved. The goal itself was a good one, with Leake sending the ball out to Charlie Smethams. When the outside-left curled a cross out of the reaches of Moger, it left Arthur Ogden to head well wide of the 'keeper and into the net. Just moments later, the 'keeper breathed a sigh of relief when the scorer crashed his shot beyond him only for the ball to strike the upright. Burnley's dominance came after two of their defenders had received early cautions. They were later joined in the book by Jimmy Turnbull for persistent fouling.

When the game restarted, the snowfall turned into a blizzard and in a series of photographs for the *Daily Mirror* of 8 March 1909, one caption reads, 'Dawson [Burnley's goalkeeper] stops Turnbull, Manchester's centre-forward. The bad state of the ground can be seen by the way Turnbull's foot has sunk into the mud.'

Burnley soon had a strong appeal for a penalty before the away side began to exert pressure on the home goal. There were big cries from among the home support for Meredith to be sent off after his heavy challenge left Jimmy McLean requiring attention. The referee, Mr H. S. Bamlett from Gateshead, ignored the demands.

With the away side attacking in greater numbers, Jeremiah (Jerry) Dawson in the Burnley goal had more to do, but he was never seriously threatened, and with the game entering the final quarter the home side looked set for a famous victory. There must have been real relief for the away side when Mr Bamlett decided the game could not continue. Only Roberts, Wall and Sandy Turnbull had played like anything like their normal game and as both soaking wet sides left the pitch, it was the side that was losing that was the happiest.

The decision of the referee was supported by the reporter in the *[Burnley] Express and Advertiser*, who wrote, 'the decision could not be regarded with a suspicion of unfairness.'

Perhaps not surprisingly, Leake disagreed and had wanted the match to continue, while Roberts for United felt the game should not have even started, making the following comment:

I think it was shame to take us out at all on a ground like that – just a sheet of ice. Men's lives are at risk, but nobody considers players as they ought to do when the elements are in question. It was not fit for a dog to be out, and all through the first half we could hardly see the ball for the snow in our eyes.

Despite United remaining in the FA Cup, the local paper was inundated with a number of rhymes that predicted their demise when the game was next held.

Play up, United, and be content
For you the Cup was never meant
The only cup that you can win
Is the butter-cup that blooms in spring

Elsewhere in the other quarter-finals, the games between Newcastle and Sunderland and Glossop and Bristol City had ended in draws, and with the Nottingham Forest versus Derby County match called off prior to kick-off, no side had made it through to the final four.

When the sides met again for a Wednesday midweek fixture, there was a crowd of 16,850 for a match played when the vast majority of local mills were still at work. This was 10,000 more than Burnley's average League gate for the season at 6,815, a sure sign of the importance of the FA Cup at the start of the twentieth century.

The size of the crowd increased steadily throughout the afternoon as more and more workers managed to leave work early to watch proceedings. It was no doubt a relief to get away from the constant banging of the machines and the heat they generated, all of which must have meant that the late arrivals would have needed a heavy, warm coat in order to be able to withstand the chill, cold wind that blew across the pitch and the rows and rows of terraced housing that gave all Burnley's streets a similar look. In 1909, the number of power looms in Burnley was just under 100,000 and it was to rise to over six figures in the years before the First World War, when the long decline of England's textiles industry began.

Many years later, a young lad, Jack Whitham, scored twice after coming on as a substitute for Sheffield Wednesday, thereby making his debut against his hometown in a match Burnley lost 7-0. It may well have been that Jack's grandfather, Thomas, was present at the Cup ties with Manchester United in 1909, against whom Jack scored a hat-trick in a 5-4 victory on 31 August 1968.

Thomas Whitham enlisted in the British Army when the First World War started and on 31 July 1917, his bravery saw him capture an enemy machine gun, together with a German officer and two soldiers. His action saved the lives of many of his Coldstream Guards Battalion. On 6 September 1917, the *Pall Mall Gazette* announced his actions had led to him being awarded the Victoria Cross, the most prestigious medal awarded for gallantry to British and Commonwealth forces. The medal did not, however, prove of great value; unemployed for considerable periods of time, the bricklayer sold it and later died from a poverty-related illness in 1924. He was only thirty-six years old.

At Turf Moor, having won the toss, Roberts chose to play with the wind behind his side. The opening exchanges were filled with misplaced passes as tension gripped the players. There was a rough challenge on James Turnbull, which saw the United forward crash heavily into the advertising boards close to the touchline. The first side to show an attacking fashion was Burnley, and Moger did well to prevent Smetham's scoring but on 15 minutes, the same player saw his shot touched on the post by the 'keeper and Ogden headed home the rebound to send hats, umbrellas and gloves into the air in celebration.

A confident home eleven then sought to press their advantage and would have done so, but Stacey made a magnificent last-ditch tackle to prevent Ogden racing clear. James Turnbull then managed a first shot for the reigning League champions before Halse equalised with a cracking drive across Dawson and in off the post to make it 1-1 on 25 minutes.

The goal that gave the away side the lead 3 minutes later was of great quality when, following a lovely cutting cross from Meredith, the ball was knocked back by Wall and finished off by James Turnbull. A pegged back home eleven were kept in the tie when Leake turned round Meredith's shot before Ogden and Stacey were fortunate to stay on the pitch after their squaring up to each other was missed by the referee. When the half-time whistle was sounded the away side were within 45 minutes of the last four.

There was a good chance for Leake on the restart, but a poor header from a corner failed to trouble Moger before the match became bogged down in the middle of the park. It was enlivened only by the assured passing of Roberts. When Wall was sent clean through, the winger was guilty of taking too long on the ball and a relieved Dawson cleared. A few minutes later, he made a fabulous save from Roberts after the United skipper had made space for a powerful shot.

Dawson holds the record for the highest number of Burnley appearances (569). After making his debut in a 3-0 win against Stockport County in April 1907, he made his final appearance at the age of 40 years 282 days on Christmas Day 1928, as the Clarets beat Liverpool 3-2. In 1914, Dawson bruised his ribs in Burnley's game prior to the FA Cup final with Liverpool and decided he might not last out the 90 minutes in the final. Dawson played almost every Burnley game when the Turf Moor team captured the League title in 1920/21.

Despite playing against the wind, it was the away side who continued to look the most likely to score again, and on 62 minutes they did so when James Turnbull made it 3-1. The home side nevertheless refused to surrender easily and Ogden reduced the arrears. In a tight finish, the away side defended heroically to set up a semi-final tie with Newcastle United.

Unlike the Magpies, Manchester United had never reached the last four of the FA Cup. The former had done so three times in the previous four seasons and had been successful in each, although they failed to win the cup on each occasion, being defeated in the final by Aston Villa in 1905, Everton in 1906 and Wolverhampton in 1908. Newcastle had beaten local rivals Sunderland 3-0 in a replay on the same day that United had won at Burnley, and the two sides met at Bramall Lane on Saturday 27 March 1909.

With most pundits believing that the winners of the tie would go on to win the cup, thousands of excursionists from Tyneside and Manchester flooded into the South Yorkshire town.

The Manchester United players had a light lunch at the Imperial Hotel before journeying to the ground.

Before the kick-off, the Newcastle fans released a dog with a black body, white neck and white feet and cheered loudly, before a little Irish terrier challenged its right to the massive ground and both were captured and removed from the field.

There was not a blade of grass on the pitch for the players for a game reported by the *Daily Mirror* on 29 March 1909:

MANCHESTER THROUGH
Newcastle United Beaten by a Goal to nothing at Sheffield
Manchester United beat Newcastle by the only goal of the match at Bramall Lane, Sheffield, on Saturday, and so for the first time in their history, qualified to take part in the final tie for the English Cup at the Crystal Palace. Judged from a spectacular point of view it was not a great game. That is there was little of the pretty combinations that both sides are famous for. The centre half for Manchester, was the best player on the field, and Colin Vietch, in the same position for Newcastle, was very little behind him. At back, too, both sides were equally well served, and the two goalkeepers never made the semblance of a mistake. Against such strong defenders it is little wonder that neither set of forwards could indulge in fancy work. At times in the first half Stewart and Wilson, on the Newcastle right, gave glimpses of delightful combination but it was ruthlessly shattered by Duckworth and Stacey.

That Manchester deserved their victory there can be no doubt, but Newcastle deserve every sympathy in the fact that centre-forward Shepherd was of little or no use to them for the greater part of the game. Before the interval, he came into violent contact with one of the Manchester defenders and had to leave the field, and although he returned for the second half, he was little more than a passenger. After a time he went to outside-left, Wilson changing over to inside-right, and Higgins went to centre, with the result that the forward line was entirely disorganised. With the wind and sun behind them in the first half, Newcastle gave their opponents some anxious moments at the start and two splendid drives by Higgins and Shepherd missed the posts by inches.

Soon, however, Duckworth, Roberts and Bell, the Manchester halves, asserted their superiority, and the Newcastle attack was almost entirely confined to individual dashes. In one of these Higgins was almost through, while his opponents were clamouring for offside, but Moger saved his shot in great style. Nor were the Manchester front line much more successful in their attempts at combination. McWilliam and Whitson dealt with Meredith in summary fashion, and McCracken gave Wall very little rope.

So at half-time nothing had been scored, and that state of affairs was a pretty good reflection of the run of the game.

The second half opened much the same as the first had finished, but when the wind freshened up and rain began to fall, Manchester kept their opponents almost entirely on the defensive. Once, from a corner, they seemed certain to score, but Lawrence affected two wonderful saves, and the danger was temporarily averted. Some 20 minutes after the interval, however, Lawrence was beaten at last. Short passing in front of the Newcastle goal left Halse with a clear opening, and, dashing in, he scored with a shot that nearly broke the netting at the back of the goal. From then on Manchester played a winning game, and when the final whistle went Newcastle had once again got so near and yet so far to lifting the coveted Cup. After this display, Manchester would start hot favourites for the final at the Palace on 24 April, and whether Bristol City or Derby County were their opponents, they were almost assured of victory.

Some 40,000 spectators watched the game, and £2,590 was taken at the gates – easily a record for a match in Sheffield.

The other semi-final finished Bristol City 1 Derby County 1, with the team from the south-west rescued by a last-gasp penalty from Willis Rippon. When the sides met again four days later at St Andrews another Rippon penalty helped his side win the replay 2-1, with Bob Hardy also scoring for the victors. The Ashton Gate club had needed nine games to make it through to the final after needing replays in the first, second, fourth and semi-final to make it through to the subsequent rounds. Just twelve goals were scored in the nine games, and of these Rippon had grabbed five.

Having lost out to Manchester United in the FA Cup, Newcastle recovered to go on and win the League title at the end of the 1908/09 season. It was the Geordies' third title success in what was the club's most successful era in a city that was a powerhouse of the Industrial Revolution from 1760 to 1840. The Newcastle and District Electric Lighting Company that was founded in 1889, opened the Neptune Bank Power Station in 1901 and from there generated the first three-phase electric power. They were also the first to supply electricity for industrial purposes rather than just lighting. This gave Tyneside industries an advantage over those in other areas.

There were four weeks between the semi-final encounter at Bramall Lane and the final at the Crystal Palace. United lost three consecutive matches, drew two and won 1-0 against Notts County. They then suffered a 3-2 defeat against Leicester Fosse, who later went out of business and were subsequently reformed as Leicester City in 1919. Two of these matches (one drawn and one lost) were against Bristol City, whose form between the semi-finals and final was not much more superior than their opponents, with just one victory – at Bank Street by 1-0 – three draws and three defeats. Neither side could therefore be said to go into the big match on a run of good form.

Only Moger, Bell, Meredith, James Turnbull and Wall played in the game against Fosse prior to the Cup final.

13

WINNING THE FA CUP

Bristol City had played their first FA Cup match in 1895/96, when they were known as Bristol South End, the name change coming in 1897. After beating Slough 5-1 at home, a 1-0 defeat at home to Marlow put the Bristol side out of the competition in the qualifying rounds. There was more success in 1898/99, and after beating three sides in the qualifying rounds, Bristol City lost 4-2 at home to Division One giants Sunderland in the first round.

In 1902/03, Bristol City, now of Division Two after gaining League entry for the start of the 1901/02 season, beat Division One side Bolton Wanderers 5-0, with Banks scoring three times. However, Bristol City had never before made it beyond the second round of the FA Cup when the 1908/09 tournament commenced.

How Bristol City Made it to the Cup Final in 1909
Southampton [H] 1-1
Southampton [A] 2-0
Bury [H] 2-2
Bury [A] 1-0
Norwich City [H] 2-0
Glossop North End [A] 0-0
Glossop North End [H] 1-0
Derby County [N] 1-1
Derby County [N] 2-1

Bristol City XI

Harry Clay enjoyed a lengthy career with his only professional club, and made 320 League and thirty-two FA Cup appearances for Bristol City. The Notts-born player was an ever-present in the 1902/03, 1903/04 and 1904/05 seasons, but when City were promoted in 1905-06 he played only eight games in 1906/07 as the Bristol side relied on William Demmery in a season in which they finished second in Division One, the club's highest ever placing. Clay returned to the side in 1908/09 and played in all but one first team match. Clay was 5 feet 9 inches tall and weighed 12st 7lbs. Clay was quick across the box, brave and kicked the ball well. He served in the Army during the First World War.

Archie Annan: After playing a single game for Sunderland, the Scotsman, a teetotaller, was signed by Bristol City from Sheffield United in May 1905 at a fee of £200. This followed the arrival at Ashton Gate of new manager Harry Thickett, a former Blade himself. After being an ever-present in his first two seasons under Thickett, Annan lost his place to new signing Bob Young in 1907/08, but in 1908/09 he recaptured his first team place and played in all ten of his side's FA Cup ties. He was a powerful player and he was awarded a joint benefit with Arthur Spear against Everton on 29 April 1911. He later coached Bristol City for five years during the 1920s.

Joe Cottle: The Bristol-born player had represented his country earlier in the 1908/09 season when he played alongside Wedlock in the England team that beat Ireland 4-0 at Bradford Park Avenue. Cottle became a regular in the Bristol City side in the early part of the 1905/06 season, and was to remain virtually an ever-present until he broke his leg during a 0-4 defeat at Preston North End on 28 January 1911. Bristol City were relegated back to the Second Division at the end of the season and Cottle left the club in the summer of 1911. He later became a local publican.

Pat Hanlin: The Scotsman made his League debut in September 1905, and was a regular in the side over the next four seasons before his place in the half-back line-up was challenged by Arthur Spear and Reuben Marr. In 1908/09, Hanlin made twenty-two League appearances, mainly at left-half, and had played in none of the nine FA Cup ties before the final. He left Bristol City when the team was relegated at the end of the 1910/11 season.

Billy Wedlock: The star of the Bristol City side, he was known as 'Fatty' or the 'India Rubber Man'. He made over 400 first-team appearances for the club. Playing at centre-half, he was a non-stop dynamo despite standing just under 5 feet 5 inches tall. He won twenty-six England caps between 1907 and 1914; his only rival for the centre-half position being Charlie Roberts. He later ran a pub for over four decades just outside Ashton Gate.

Arthur Spear played for local clubs before moving to Bristol City in 1904, where as a utility player accustomed to playing in a number of different positions, he was a regular in the side over the following six seasons. He played in all ten FA Cup ties in 1910. He was later a publican for over three decades.

Fred Staniforth: City signed the Yorkshireman from Mexborough Town in July 1906, and he replaced Walter Bennett at outside-right the following season. In 1907/08, he was part of a regular forward line that also comprised Billy Maxwell, Gilligan, Burton and Hilton. Staniforth played in all ten of the Bristol City Cup ties in 1909. He joined Grimsby Town when Bristol City were relegated in 1911.

Bob Hardy: Tricky on the ball, Hardy stood just 5 feet 6 inches tall and won one cap for England at amateur level. Hardy scored his only FA Cup goal for Bristol City in the semi-final success against Derby County at St Andrews.

Sammy Gilligan was top scorer for Bristol City in the League in 1907/08 and 1908/09 with sixteen and ten goals respectively. The Scotsman was a lively attacker who loved taking on defences. He was a good dribbler of the ball, a good passer of the ball out to the wings and possessed a powerful shot. He later joined Liverpool and scored sixteen goals in forty-one appearances before becoming player-manager at Gillingham. He later emigrated to Vancouver, Canada and lived into his nineties.

Andy Burton: Another Scotsman who featured regularly for Bristol City under manager Harry Thickett between 1905 and 1910. He scored thirteen goals from thirty-four League appearances as the regular inside left during the 1906/07 season, when City finished runners-up to Newcastle United. He scored eight League goals in 1908/09 and played in all ten FA Cup ties, scoring against Bury and Norwich City in the early rounds. Burton moved to Everton in July 1911 and was still playing for East Fife in the Scottish Second Division in 1921/22. Tricky on the ball, he could annoy supporters by apparently hanging on to it for too long.

Frank Hilton played for Doncaster St Legers before signing for Bristol City, where he scored just once in the FA Cup in a 2-1 defeat away to Grimsby Town in 1907/08. He stood just 5-foot 7-inches tall and weighed 10st 5lbs.

Harry Thickett: The Bristol City manager was one of the best players of his generation. He was twice capped for England and was a major part of the famous Sheffield United side at the turn of the century, where he won a League winners' medal in 1897/98, and two FA Cup winners' medals in 1899 and 1902, with a runners-up medal in 1901. The right-back moved to Bristol City at the end of the 1903/04 season and replaced Sam Hollis as manager in March 1905. He soon after took the crucial decision to re-sign Billy Wedlock, who had left the club in 1901. He secured promotion in 1905/06, and took City to second place in Division One in 1906/07. After the 1909 FA Cup final, his side began to slide and his tenure as manager came to an end following a 1-0 away defeat to Notts County in October 1910.

On St George's Day, the *Daily Mirror* reported (perhaps wrongly as Sandy Turnbull had yet to be declared so) that all of Manchester United's players were fit for the big day twenty-four hours later, but Bristol City had lost Willis Rippon, their centre-forward, and right-back Rueben Marr, to injuries. Their replacements were to be Frank Hilton and Pat Hanlin, whose appearance was likely to be his last for the Ashton Gate club as he had not been re-engaged for the 1909/10 season. Inside-left Andy Burton had also failed to be granted a new contract by the Bristol board, but in the event he eventually re-signed and was still playing for City before football was suspended because of the war. By that time, City had dropped down into Division Two following relegation at the end of the 1910/11 season.

Supporters of the south-west club were convinced of their success. They were pointing towards the Old Moore prophetic almanac for 1909 that had prophesised that a side called City would win the Cup. If Bristol City did capture the trophy they would be the first from that part of the country to do so.

The *Daily Mirror* the following day (24 April) was predicting that Bristol City would not allow Manchester United to play 'their clever, brilliant football ... thus we are likely to see a hard, dour battle, and not much scoring.' It was noted that the sides had met twice since securing their places in the final, and only one goal had been scored.

The reporter did, though, feel that the large Crystal Palace pitch would favour United's more expansive wing-play, and he pointed out that Wall had scored two in the recent 2-0 England victory there against Scotland, a feat that rightly earned him the Man of the Match award. Although, it appears not to have played a part in the eventual Manchester United victory, the northern side did have a distinct height advantage with only Annan in the Bristol City side being as tall as 5 feet 10 inches, whereas Bell, Stacey, Meredith and Halse were all 5 feet 10 inches and James Turnbull was 5 feet 11 inches and Roberts even taller. Moger in goal was well over 6 feet tall.

The *Bristol Echo*, which cost one halfpenny, had wished for heavy rain so 'the ground would be churned into that mud we know our players so revel in'.

The *Bristol Echo* and *Daily Mirror* were among the 126 press men (they were almost certainly all men) present at the 1909 FA Cup final. This is around a third of the 400 from the press who would cover an FA Cup final today at Wembley. There was, of course, no live TV coverage, but Pathe News, who had first covered the FA Cup final in 1901, were there to film the major events and show them in cinemas across the country in the days following the final. In 1909, the producer of newsreels and documentaries was based in Paris. In 1910, Charles Pathe opened a newsreel office in Wardour Street, London. Newsreels were shown in cinemas, and up until 1928 they were silent. Pathe ended cinema newsreels in 1970 as they could no longer compete with television.

The *Daily Mirror* also carried a lengthy account of the final that started at 3.30 p.m., and believed that the gate for it of 71,401 – the lowest since the 61,374 at the 1904 final between Manchester City and Bolton Wanderers – could largely be accounted for by the absence of 'the Cockney element.' Londoners had chosen to miss the final and instead view the games between Tottenham Hotspur and Bradford Park Avenue and Clapton Orient and Bolton Wanderers. These attracted a combined attendance of 36,000 for matches that went a long way to deciding who won promotion to Division One at the end of the season.

The national paper felt that Manchester United 'deserved their victory but Bristol had enough chances in the second half to have won, but failed to take advantage of them'. Bristol had kicked into a strong wind in the first half and played with it behind them in the second. Surrounded by cameras and cinematographs, Charlie Roberts had won the toss and chosen to play with the wind behind him in the initial 45 minutes.

To great cheers, Bristol had entered the field of play first at 3.11 p.m., and was swiftly followed by Manchester United. A metropolitan band that had for some time enlivened proceedings played 'Rule Britannia' and the National Anthem, both of which were sung lustily by the expectant crowd. The latter song had many spectators believing that the Prince of Wales had joined the crowd but it simply signalled the end of the band's performance. Also absent was Lord Kinnaird, the FA's president, who wanted nothing to do with Manchester United's Players' Union. Kinnaird would, in fact, end up taking permanent possession of the trophy United were set to win. Manchester United were to make a replica of it and present it to J. H. Davies, and an angered FA replaced the original and handed the FA Cup to Kinnaird.

With both sides normally wearing red, they lined up in changed colours, United wearing white jerseys with a red rose on the chest. City wore royal blue jerseys with the Bristol coat of arms on the chest. According to the *Daily Mirror,* the change in colours had the effect of making the crowd, among who were many more followers of United than City, rather drab as few wore their side's colours. Fans of both sides had the chance to remember the momentous day by purchasing a match programme with team line-ups and a children's coupon worth a shilling (5 pence). There are no records of how many were sold, but in 2012 one of them fetched a world-record price of £23,500 when it was bought by a UK collector. A similar programme was sold for £16,000 in late 2013.

Some of the crowd had arrived four hours before kick-off in an attempt to get the best view possible of the day's events from the grassy banks – which were covered by small gravel terraces – that dominated the giant enclosure, which staged its first final in 1895 and its last in 1914. The *Manchester Evening News* on Cup final day itself had a photograph prior to their travel south from the London Road Station in Manchester of Rocca's Brigade with red-and-white caps and coloured brollies. One fan was dressed in a red-and-white striped suit. The Brigade was named in honour of Louis Rocca junior, the son of a prominent local Italian ice cream businessman.

This wasn't the first time Manchester had drawn inspiration from Italians. Many of the architectural developments in the city in the nineteenth century relied heavily on medieval and Renaissance Italy, including the Manchester Athenaeum, the Free Trade Hall, the Town Hall, Victoria University and the John Rylands Library.

The Salford-born architect Thomas Worthington (1826–1909) described Manchester in 1876 as 'the Florence of the nineteenth century' when he addressed the Manchester Society of Architects.

Louis Rocca had been involved with Newton Heath in its formative years and at one time served as the club's grounds man. He claimed that when it was proposed to change the name of the club in 1902, he had suggested Manchester United. Rocca maintained his association with Manchester United over many years, and his finest hour came when he helped persuade his friend Matt Busby, who was born in the summer of 1909, to become the club's manager at the end of the Second World War. Rocca died in 1950, just two years after Manchester United won the FA Cup for the second time in the club's history, beating Blackpool 4-2 at Wembley in a match rated one of the finest staged there.

Those fans who arrived by train in 1909 waited until the heavy overnight rain eased off around 7.00 a.m. before setting out to visit – almost certainly for the first and possibly only times in their lives – notable London locations such as the House of Commons, Westminster Abbey, St Paul's and the Tower of London.

Few may have considered visiting the Stock Exchange or touring the City of London financial districts, which even then were dominating the British economy such that whereas Britain had a £137 million deficit in its balance of commodity trade between 1906 and 1910, it had a £140 million surplus on its international commercial and financial business transactions.

The *Daily Mirror* noted that the Bristol City side lined up as expected but that 'after all, Turnbull was able to play', ensuring the Manchester United side was at its strongest. The Monday edition of the *Manchester Evening News* reported: 'Turnbull, who, after being declared unfit to play ... played only because of his determination. He was suffering severely after the first hour, but though his thigh still causes him pain, he declares that he is fully repaid for all the troubles he went through to take part in the match.'

'Sandy played,' said Mr Mangnall, 'though the trainer and the specialist and almost everybody agreed that he would not be able to do so. He promised that if he went on the field he would not come off until the match was over, and he fully redeemed his pledge. We knew he would, and it was the confidence the directors had in him that induced them at the last moment to give him the opportunity – a decision they cannot now regret.'

It was the side from the south-west who had the best chance when the game kicked off, but Gilligan, not for the last time, fired wide after being found by Staniforth. It took some time for the United full- and half-backs to become accustomed to the strong wind, and their initial efforts to find their forwards foundered when the ball was kicked too strongly. The side from the north-west were then grateful to Moger for preserving their goal when the 'keeper, using every inch of his 6-foot 2-inch frame, made a brilliant save from a fine Hardy drive.

This let off seemed to inspire the reigning League champions, who pushed their opponents back on the defensive and forced a series of corners that Bristol City defended valiantly. The *Bristol Echo* report that appeared on the evening of the match praised 'United's three grand halves behind the forwards', and it was a fact that of the two centre-halves on display, Roberts was the more influential in this particular tussle.

As the halfway point approached, Roberts was noticeably involved in a United attack and when Meredith and Halse combined, the latter hit a powerful shot off the crossbar. Fastening on to the rebound, Sandy Turnbull, from close-in, showed good control and drove the ball well wide of Clay and into the Bristol net to make it 1-0. The joyous cries of Lancastrians could be heard right round the massive enclosure.

For the next few minutes it was all the losing side could do to hang on and the scorer almost made it 2-0, Turnbull firing narrowly wide after nodding a Meredith cross over the Bristol City defence before firing only just wide. With Wedlock at his defensive best, popping up everywhere, the side managed by Harry Thickett worked tirelessly to stay in the match.

A chance of an equaliser was then thwarted by a cynical piece of play. It came after Burton dribbled past Roberts and Stacey and as he raced towards goal, he was brought down by Hayes. Today it would be a straight red, but the United left-back was not even spoken to by the referee, and the resulting free-kick was hit over the bar by Wedlock. Burton did then manage a shot but it was easily saved by Moger, and the winning side again pushed forward and continued to dictate the pace of the game.

Yet when half-time arrived and their side had failed to take advantage, many Manchester United fans must have feared they had failed to build a big enough lead for what seemed sure to be a Bristol City wind-assisted onslaught in the second period. Following the 10-minute interval, Manchester United's chances looked a lot less rosy when Hayes was forced to leave the field for treatment after suffering an early second-half severe strain injury, and although the left-back was able to return, he was a passenger for the rest of the match. The injury forced Manchester United to change their formation, with Duckworth dropping back to full-back and Halse going to right half-back with Hayes occupying the inside-right position. Duckworth's display was to win him the praise of the *Daily Mirror,* whose match heading described a 'Great Display by Duckworth'.

Even so, the defender was powerless to prevent Gilligan dashing clear of the United rearguard and as he moved to strike the ball towards goal, Moger dived full length to bravely scoop the ball off the City forward's toe. Burton, too, was then guilty of failing to shoot when well placed. With their followers urging them on, Bristol City now enjoyed the majority of possession, although every time the ball was cleared Meredith and Wall continued to remain real dangers, and the tussle between the latter and Annan was one of the most pleasing features of the whole match.

With time fast running out, Stacey's header bounced off Gilligan, who then sent a pass to Hilton. With only Moger to beat, the Bristol player shot weakly across goal, failing to bring the scores level.

As the match moved towards its conclusion, the tension had clearly got to the players and there were a number of challenges that the *Daily Mirror* commented were 'unworthy of the players'. They felt James Turnbull was especially fortunate not to have been dismissed. When the final whistle was sounded, Manchester United had captured the FA Cup for the first time by beating Bristol City 1-0.

The *Daily Mirror* reporter praised Duckworth, Stacey and Roberts, especially for his supremacy over Gilligan, and also felt that Meredith and Wall had played excellently. Moger's diving save, it was said, would be talked about for many years afterwards. Both Turnbulls were rated as only moderate, but 'Sandy got his goal and so justified his inclusion'. It was his – and Meredith's – second success in the Cup final, having previously won it with Manchester City in 1904.

After the game, an ode to the scorer was penned and became popular among the winning club's followers.

Why we thought you were 'crocked' Dashing Sandy,
That to fame your road was blocked, Hard Lines Sandy,
But you came up to the scratch,
Made an effort for THE match...
When Halse hit the shiv-ring bar, Lucky Sandy,
There were groans near and far, Deep ones, Sandy,
But the ball was on the bound,
And your boot was safe and sound,
When the net your great shot found, Champion Sandy.
For the score was but one up – not much Sandy?
But the Bristol boys worked hard
Though their efforts were ill-starred
Give a cheer then with the band, For them Sandy.

Whereas the Bristol full- and half-backs had all played very well, the *Daily Mirror* felt only Hardy in the forward line played anything like his normal form. Gilligan was felt to be 'an absolute failure' and Hilton had missed the easiest chance of the entire 90 minutes.

After the game finished, Lord Charles Beresford, who was a British Admiral and commanded the Mediterranean Fleet between 1905 and 1907, presented the Cup and medals to the successful side from the pavilion on the west side of the ground. He said it was a gallant game that had been played fairly and in a sportsmanlike fashion. He felt that football encouraged the best characteristics of the British race and the game should be, as it was in the armed forces, encouraged. As they were presented with their medals, one of the winning side wished the Admiral success with the Navy in the future.

The victorious side then became the guests of (Sir) George Robey for the next 24 to 36 hours. The English music hall comedian, singer and actor was known as the 'Prime Minister of Mirth' and for his song 'If You Were the Only Girl in the World'. He was a big football fan and although born in London, he had a strong affection for Manchester United. After visiting the Alhambra Music Hall, the team and the FA Cup went to see Robey at the Pavilion Music Hall. With some of the players lost en route, Robey had some men from Manchester – who were sitting in the nearby Trocadero theatre – join them on stage. No one seemed to notice that the United 'players' included a publican, bookmaker, a builder and greengrocer! The following day, Robey invited the players and directors to join him at his home in Finchley for Sunday lunch.

In the meantime, the vast majority of fans had travelled back north. After hardly sleeping in over 24 hours, many had been totally shattered after the match and the newspapers reported how they had occupied the station floors in the hours up to their departure. The Manchester United side could expect a more luxurious trip home and were set to depart from St Pancras on the Tuesday noon express that was due to arrive at Manchester Central station at 3.30 p.m.

The *Manchester Evening News*, Tuesday 27 April 1909
UNITED'S HOME-COMING
Our London correspondent telegraphs:

The last I saw of the Association Football Cup was as it was waved in the air by its proud possessor, Mr. Mangnall, the secretary of the Manchester United Football Club, as the noon train sped out of St Pancras Station en route for Manchester.

The team had a most pleasant experience this weekend. Yesterday afternoon the players and those who have been staying with them had a drive out to Hampstead Heath – 'Appy Ampstead' as Londoners delight to call it.

It was the real regret that many of the party returned to the North. Some of them told me that they only wished they could live here altogether; these, it is needless to say were the ladies of the party. Boxes packed away into two saloons which were occupied by the party bore the names of many well-known London shops.

The players left the hotel shortly after eleven o'clock. Charlie Roberts and Duckworth walked to St Pancras, but the bulk of the party travelled to the station in omnibuses belonging to the Imperial Hotel. A small crowd gathered round the players as they departed, and raised a cheer and a cry of 'Good Old Manchester.'

The Scene at St Pancras

On the platform there was a scene of bustle. Some photographs, which had been taken during the later stages of the training at Chingford, were distributed by the photographer who had developed them. It was as much the porters could do to get the players and their friends onto the train, and the ticket collector was at his wits' end to get the small bits of paste board that entitled them to travel on the train.

At last the signal for departure was given by the stationmaster, and the train began to move. The crowd that had gathered round the carriage gave voice to their feelings, and cheers and cries of 'Good Old Manchester' were heard all round. Mr Mangnall was carrying the Cup in his hand, and waved it at the crowd as it was rapidly being carried away on the journey to its resting place for the next twelve months.

Great Crowds At Central Station

An hour before the time the train was due to arrive at Central Station, large crowds of people assembled outside the station and behind the barricades of the approach leading to the platform at which the London train usually comes in. The great majority wore the United colours and an ice cream merchant attracted considerable attention with his huge red and white umbrella and his similarly coloured barrow. Gutter merchants who did good business with memory cards of Bristol City came in for good humoured badinage, while the United favours attached to a cardboard representation of the English cup sold like hot cakes.

Scenes Outside Town Hall

Long before the team was due to arrive at the Town Hall, Albert Square was crowded with people, and when they did arrive there were several thousand anxiously waiting to see the victorious players. The police had great difficulty in keeping the crowd in order, and barricades had been erected right round the square. Great enthusiasm prevailed even before the party for the station put in an appearance.

The Arrival

There were wild scenes of enthusiasm, with the greatest pressure being just outside the station, where a strong body of police had considerable difficulty in keeping back the crowd. Five waggonettes, gaily decorated with red-and-white banners and ribbons, were in waiting, along with two outstanding members of the St Joseph's Industrial School Band. The arrival of Rocca's Brigade, gaudily dressed in the colours of the United club, was the signal for an outburst of cheering. At first they weren't any more successful than many who made improper demands for admission to the platform, but eventually, amidst much uproar, the waggonette was allowed to pass through.

They had not been there many minutes when the London train hove in sight, and amid a scene of wild enthusiasm, Mr Mangnall emerged carrying the cup on high, followed by the players, their wives and other people who had travelled from the Metropolis.

A Great Scramble

The band struck up 'See, the Conquering Hero Comes', and there was a great scramble by the crowd, which had been permitted to enter the platform to reach the players.

Some were carried shoulder high, and ultimately they were comfortably seated in the third waggonette. To the accompaniment of enlivening strains of music by the boys of St Joseph's School, the procession moved out of the station, and its appearance was signalled by a tremendous outburst of cheering.

Sticks were waved, hats were thrown in the air, and the enthusiasm was unbounded when Roberts, carrying the trophy, came into view. The police had their work cut out to prevent the crowd 'rushing' the waggonette, but happily the vehicle passed along the approach without mishap.

A Triumphal Progress

The crowds were almost equally as dense by the Midland Hotel, and the scenes of enthusiasm were renewed as the waggonette passed on its triumphal progress along Mount Street to Albert Square, which was densely packed with people eager to catch a glimpse of the victorious team.

Civic Reception

At the Town Hall the teams were conducted to the private room of the Lord Mayor, where they were received by Alderman Holt. The officials and players were introduced to the Lord Mayor by Mr J. H. Davies, who thanked Alderman Holt for receiving them. He gave the Lord Mayor many interesting facts concerning the English cup, which Alderman Holt examined closely.

The Lord Mayor expressed pleasure in welcoming the team, and said their performance was a very creditable one. It showed that they had grit and commonsense, and that they obeyed their orders.

They had won the cup in a fair and honourable manner, and he hoped they would do it again next year – (hear, hear) – and that they would win it a third time. He mentioned the fact that the club had helped charitable projects, and he thanked them for their aid, especially in connection with the Lord Mayor's Fund. It would be well for them to bear in mind that whatever they did, it must be of the best.

Mr J. J. Bentley, in moving a vote of thanks to the Lord Mayor, remarked that thirty years ago he fought for the Cup as a player, but this was the first time he had been connected with a club that had won the trophy.

A Tour of the City

After leaving the Town Hall, the party made a tour of the city, passing along John Dalton Street, Deangate, St Mary's Gate, Market Street, Oldham Street and on to the ground at Clayton.

There was a crowd of just 10,000 inside Bank Street for the Arsenal game that kicked off just minutes after the successful Cup-winning side arrived at 6.00 p.m., and which was easily won by the visitors 4-1. The FA Cup was displayed from the president's box and after the game there was another celebratory dinner, which many players absented themselves from.

1908/09 Records
All home games at Bank Street

August
QPR [N] Charity Shield 4-0

September
Preston North End [A] 3-0
Bury [H] 2-1
Middlesbrough [H] 6-3
Manchester City [A] 2-1
Liverpool [H] 3-2

October
Bury [A] 2-2
Sheffield United [H] 2-1

Aston Villa [A] 1-3
Nottingham Forest [H] 2-2
Sunderland [A] 1-6

November
Chelsea [H] 0-1
Blackburn Rovers [A] 3-1
Bradford City [H] 2-0
Sheffield Wednesday [H] 3-1

December
Everton [A] 2-3
Leicester City [H] 4-2
Arsenal [A] 1-0
Newcastle United [A] 1-2
Newcastle United [H] 1-0

January
Notts County [H] 4-3
Preston North End [H] 0-2
Middlesbrough [A] 0-5
Brighton [H] FA Cup 1-0
Manchester City [H] 3-1
Liverpool [A] 1-3

February
Everton [H] FA Cup 1-0
Sheffield United [A] 0-0
Blackburn Rovers [H] FA Cup 6-1
Nottingham Forest [A] 0-2

March
Burnley [A] FA Cup 0-1 (abandoned)
Burnley [A] FA Cup 3-2
Chelsea [A] 1-1
Sunderland [H] 2-2
Blackburn Rovers [H] 0-3
Newcastle United [N] FA Cup 1-0
Aston Villa [H] 0-2

April
Sheffield Wednesday [A] 0-2
Bristol City [H] 0-1
Everton [H] 2-2
Bristol City [A] 0-0
Notts County [A] 1-0
Leicester City [A] 2-3
Bristol City [N] FA Cup 1-0
Arsenal [H] 1-4
Bradford City [A] 0-1

Manchester United finished in thirteenth place with 37 points from 38 games. The home record was won 10, drawn 3 and lost 6, with 37 goals for and 33 conceded. Away from home, 5 victories were recorded with 10 defeats and 4 draws. Twenty-one goals were scored and 35 conceded. United finished 16 points behind League champions Newcastle United, and just 3 points above the relegation zone.

The following were signed to play for Manchester United during the season:

George Hayes: Full-back Hayes returned to Manchester United in the summer of 1908. He had debuted in the first team for Newton Heath against Walsall on 25 February 1901, and played regularly there afterwards. However, after breaking his leg in his first reserve match against Liverpool in September 1905, he spent a long time out of action and joined Brentford in May 1907. His form was such that he returned north to his hometown the following summer and he was to appear in all of the FA Cup games in the 1909 success. Hayes was a non-smoker and abstained from drink. He represented the Football League against the Scottish League in February 1910, but when he failed to establish himself at the start of the following season, he was allowed to transfer over the Pennines to join Bradford City.

George Livingstone: After moving to Rangers in November 1906, when the ban on Manchester City players was lifted, the Scotsman returned to Manchester in January 1909 and was to stay at United for the next six seasons, spending the final four as player-coach for the Central League reserve team. He switched from playing at inside right in his first season and a half to half-back in 1910/11, during which he made ten League starts.

Oscar Linkson: Signed in the summer of 1908, Linkson debuted against Nottingham Forest on 24 October 1908. He was to go on and make fifty-nine first team appearances before moving to play for Shelbourne in 1913. He was killed in action during the war, one of three United players to suffer such a fate – the others being Sandy Turnbull and Pat McGuire, an amateur reserve player.

Appearances

	League	FA Cup
Moger	36	6
Wall	34	6
Duckworth	33	6
Meredith	34	4
Stacey	32	6
Halse	29	6
Roberts	27	6
Hayes	22	6
J. Turnbull	22	6
Bell	20	6
A. Turnbull	19	6
Downie	23	-
Bannister	16	-
Livingstone	11	2
Picken	13	-
Linkson	10	-
Curry	8	-
Burgess	4	-
Ford	4	-
Hardman	4	-
Hulme	3	-
Christie	2	-
Holden	2	-
McGillivray	2	-
Payne	2	-
Wilcox	2	-
Berry	1	-
Donnelly	1	-
Quinn	1	-
Thomson	1	-

Scorers

	League	FA Cup
J. Turnbull	17	5
Halse	14	4
Wall	11	-
A. Turnbull	5	4
Livingstone	3	-
Picken	3	-
Bell	3	-
Bannister	1	-
Payne	1	-
Roberts	1	-

14

ANOTHER BRIGHT START
TO A SEASON

The FA Cup holders started their League season on 1 September 1909. It was a Wednesday and a crowd of 12,000 was inside Bank Street to witness a 1-0 home success over Bradford City. Wall scored the only goal and there was a debut at inside-right for Sam Blott, who had been signed from Southend in the summer. Livingstone, though, was to be back for the next game three days later at home to Bury. Blott was to make just nineteen appearances in the four years he was at Manchester United. Two James Turnbull goals saw Bury beaten 2-0, and there was a third consecutive home success when Notts County were beaten 2-1 on the Bank Holiday Monday.

Five days later there was a 40,000-strong crowd inside White Hart Lane for an eagerly awaited match with Spurs, FA Cup winners in 1901 and a side that had won promotion at the end of its first season of League football in 1908/09. Tottenham had managed to raise the funds to buy the land for the ground from the brewers Charringtons in 1905, and they constructed a new main stand in 1909. In the their first season of football in Division One, Tottenham were to average 27,560 at the turnstiles, just behind the best supported club, Chelsea, who averaged 28,545.

Having started their season with two away games (both defeats) the game with United was Tottenham Hotspur's – the word Hotspur is believed to be that of 'Harry Hotspur' of Shakespeare's *Henry IV* – first top-flight home match.

Playing at centre-forward for the home side was Walter Tull. In an era when there were few challenges to racist abuse, Tull was known as

'Darkie'. He was born to an English mother and West Indian father in Kent on 28 April 1888. Tull's grandmother had been a slave in Barbados and he was to be the second black player in English football.

Tull made just eighteen first-team appearances for Tottenham, but later played over 100 times for Northampton before he enrolled in the Army where he became the first black man to be commissioned as an infantry officer. This was despite the 1914 Manual of Military Law specifically excluding 'Negroes or Mulattos' from exercising control. After fighting in the Battle of the Somme alongside fellow footballers in the Footballers' Battalion, Tull fought in Italy in 1917/18, and was mentioned in dispatches for his gallantry while leading his company of twenty-six men on a raiding party in enemy territory. On his return to France, he was killed in action on 25 March 1918 during the Spring Offensive on the Western Front. His body was never recovered.

Sandy Turnbull was also killed in the war. He played for Manchester United during the 1914/15 season, but afterwards he was found guilty of conspiring with two other Manchester United players – Enoch West and Arthur Whalley – and four from Liverpool – Jackie Sheldon, Tom Fairfoul, Tom Miller and Bob Pursell – to fix the result of the game at Old Trafford on Good Friday 1915. Chester player Lol Cook was also found to have been party to the conspiracy, which undoubtedly involved more than those who were permanently banned for playing or participating in football management.

The 2-0 home success helped the victors retain their place in the top flight when League football resumed in 1919/20. It also, by various twists and turns, helped Arsenal, who finished sixth in Division Two in 1914/15, to gain promotion. Ironically, Turnbull did not even play in the match, the events of which were similar to the game at Bank Street against Notts County in April 1908, when there was a missed penalty.

With football suspended in the summer of 1915, Sandy enrolled in early 1916 and joined the Footballers' Battalion of the Middlesex Regiment. He later transferred to the 8th Battalion of the East Surrey Regiment. Because his army records were destroyed during the Blitz in London in the Second World War, no one knows if he was one of those from the Battalion who dribbled footballs into the Battle of the Somme on 1 July 1916. Probably not, as most were quickly killed.

Although the war was on, that didn't mean class differences were overlooked, and although the daily diary of the East Surreys has survived, we know little about what Sandy was up to as it only mentions officers. Yet it would surely not be coincidental that the 8th swept all before them in the divisional championship in the spring of 1917.

On 3 May 1917, the 8th East Surreys stormed the little village of Chérisy, around 10 miles east of Arras. This was virtually open countryside and most of the soldiers involved must have feared the worst. The attack commenced at 3.45 a.m. and although the initial objective was achieved, a German counter-attack soon had the amateur British soldiers – who were really only trained for trench warfare and could barely use their rifles – fleeing back to where they had come from. According to the British official history, there was 'bewilderment among the British infantry on finding itself in the open and its inability to withstand resolute counter attack'.

Over 500 8th Surreys were in the attack, and in the rout that followed 90 were killed, 175 were wounded (there is no record of any subsequent fatalities among them) and over 100 were captured during the withdrawal. At first no one knew what had happened to Sandy and his death remained unrecorded in The *Manchester Guardian*, a paper that had often reported his football exploits. In his hometown, the now defunct *Kilmarnock Herald* reported his possible death on 18 May 1917 under the headline 'Former Hurlford footballer: wounded prisoner of war.' The subsequent report spoke of his bravery and of him being seriously injured.

Once the war finished Turnbull's commanding officer, Capt. C. J. Lonergan, who had been one of those captured by the Germans, wrote to Turnbull's wife to say how disappointed he was that he had not been heard of and commented that he was 'my best Non Commissioned Officer ... he had been hit through the leg early on in the fight ... it was so swollen I ordered him back to the dressing station. He pleaded so hard, however, to be allowed to stay on until we gained our objective I gave way. Sandy was in command of a platoon. The men would simply go anywhere with him.'

Lonergan had seen the Lance Sergeant alive during the withdrawal and, at first, believed he had made it back to the houses the British had taken during the initial attack. He felt that the footballer must have been 'sniped' by a German. It is likely that Turnbull was buried in a shallow grave that would have been obliterated in the heavy fighting that followed. Lonergan recommended that Turnbull be given the 'highest distinction possible. He certainly deserves it.'

Turnbull is listed on the curving colonnade monument to 'the missing' in the massive British war cemetery in Arras. The soldiers are listed in rank order and A. Turnbull is under the section for Lance Sergeants.

After the war ended, it was agreed to pardon those footballers who were involved in fixing the Easter 1915 match because they had enlisted in the armed forces. Only two were unable to resume – Sandy Turnbull was one and the other was Enoch West, who despite joining the armed forces angered the authorities by insisting he was innocent and unsuccessfully suing for libel.

In 1935, Sir Frederick Wall published his book on *50 Years of Football 1884–1934.* In this he devoted a number of pages to Vivian Woodward, an England amateur who played for Spurs and Chelsea from 1901 to 1915, and who captained the successful Great Britain football side at the 1908 and 1912 Olympics. Woodward starred in 67 amateur internationals and also scored 29 goals in 23 full England internationals. Wall felt 'Woodward was as dangerous near goal with his head as anyone other than Alec Turnbull ('Sandy') and Dean, of Everton, in these latter days'.

The game was considered important enough for the *Daily Mirror* to feature it in its photographic section of the following Monday's paper. There were four photographs in all and one shows Moger unsuccessfully advancing off his line to try and prevent centre-half Daniel Steel from scoring from the penalty spot; both of the home side's goals on the day came from the spot and the same player. The photograph also provided its readers with some understanding of the layout of White Hart Lane as it also captured the standing crowd behind the goal and on the opposite bank that fans of today would know as 'the Shelf'.

The game – which attracted receipts of £1,021 – got off to a sensational start when United scored twice in the first 5 minutes, and both James Turnbull and Wall's successful efforts were the result of some brilliant attacking play. The home side were able to hang on and following their two goals, they pressed for a winner only to be denied by a magnificent display by Moger in the United goal. The *Daily Mirror* report was extremely complimentary, concluding that 'this match was a brilliant display of fast football'. The draw marked the first point achieved by Spurs at the highest-level of English football.

The away side had started with seven points from a possible eight, but the next four games were to bring just two, both from draws. The final match of the four was away to Liverpool and the away side were missing Moger, his damaged thigh giving an opportunity to Elijah Round, the ex-Oldham 'keeper, who made the first of only two appearances for United. The previous weekend had seen United draw 1-1 with champions Newcastle United, a game in which Joe Ford had played well and he retained his place at the expense of Wall.

Jack Parkinson opened the scoring for Liverpool after just 7 minutes, a feat accompanied by enormous cheers. Parkinson was to give Charlie Roberts the run around for the entire 90 minutes, and it was the same player who made it 2-0 when he rushed in with the ball to beat Round. Parkinson was to score thirty League goals in 1909/10, finishing as top scorer in the First Division. He was denied a hat-trick just before half-time when Round saved his shot with his legs.

Having survived a battering in the first period, Ernest Mangnall's side stunned the hosts with two quick goals at the start of the second half. First Sandy Turnbull netted from the spot after Halse was fouled, and he then made it 2-2 after he scored from a Meredith corner.

Round had drawn great applause when he saved a John MacDonald shot early in the second period, but the 'keeper was left helpless when MacDonald floated over a superb cross that left him and the defenders in front of him and a towering Jimmy Stewart powered a header home that produced a roar that would have been heard from miles away. A determined United charge then silenced the Anfield crowd for the remaining 15 minutes of the match, but when the referee sounded the final whistle, the away side had lost 3-2 and now had nine points from their opening eight matches of the 1909/10 season.

Moger and Wall both returned to the starting line-up for the following fixture at home to Aston Villa, and after Sandy Turnbull missed a penalty, he atoned for his error by opening the scoring in a 2-0 win in which Halse netted the second. A crowd of 20,000 watched the encounter, well under half the number present when the sides had clashed at Bank Street in the 1906 FA Cup. This produced receipts of £1,460, but with another 10,000 locked out and many inside unable to see much of the game the affair demonstrated how inadequate United's ground was for staging big matches. The summer of 1906 witnessed major ground improvements at Everton, Liverpool, Birmingham and Blackburn Rovers, but Bank Street remained just as uncomfortable, downright dangerous and unhealthy for spectators and players as before.

A single Wall goal at Bramall Lane saw the visitors beat Sheffield United 1-0, before the same player repeated his feat the following weekend when Woolwich Arsenal was beaten 1-0 at Bank Street. Sandy Turnbull's fiery temperament had seen him lash out at an opponent during the match in Yorkshire, and his dismissal, combined with his previous poor disciplinary record, resulted in him being suspended for six matches.

A fourth consecutive success was recorded in a 3-2 victory at Burnden Park on 6 November 1909. The away side had Moger to thank for a late penalty save, but deserved their success in a game in which Meredith was outstanding but his display was bettered by the Bolton 'keeper, Edmondson, who constantly defied the United forwards. Homer scored twice and Halse once for the successful side.

Prior to the next match, at home to Chelsea, it was reported that captain Charlie Roberts had received clearance from the FA for a benefit match and that Manchester United would be allowed to make up the receipts to £500 in the event of bad weather reducing the attendance at the agreed game. Two second-half goals from Sandy Turnbull and Wall helped the hosts win 2-0, a fifth consecutive success that raised real hopes of another title charge.

Such hopes, though, were to prove misplaced as of the next six matches, only one was won and the rest were lost. Two penalties by Bradshaw helped Blackburn Rovers win 3-2 at Ewood Park before a 40,000-strong crowd that paid record receipts of £1,200.

There was then a remarkable game at home to Nottingham Forest, whose eighteen goals had all been scored by Enoch West and Grenville Morris, a Welsh international dubbed the 'Prince of the Inside-Lefts' and who away from football was a fine tennis and chess player.

Both men had scored for their side in what was another amazing match in 1909. Playing at home to Leicester Fosse on 21 April, the Forest side were desperate to avoiding joining their already relegated opponents in the Second Division the following season. With the remaining sides at the bottom tightly packed, a victory by a few goals would also help Forest with their goal average.

The game ended in a 12-0 success for Forest, with West scoring three and Morris two. There were also hat-tricks for Spouncer and Hooper. Following a protest from other relegation-threatened clubs, a League inquiry was held and it later transpired that two days before the game, the Fosse side had attended the wedding of teammate Turner and the celebrations that followed lasted until the early hours of the day of the match against Forest. No punishment was awarded against Leicester and Forest stayed up. The score line is the most one-sided in the history of top flight football in England.

At the start of the game in November 1909, there was controversy when Meredith was heavily barged over the line and into the advertising hoarding behind the pitch by Wolfe. Morris, Meredith's Welsh international colleague opened the scoring, but after 6 minutes the game was tied following a Halse equaliser.

At this point, Stacey was so badly injured that he was forced to leave the field, after which the away side had five shots and scored with all five to take the score up to 6-1 in their favour. Moger's task was not helped by the fading light that on another day might have seen the abandonment of the match. A late Wall goal made it 6-2, but the result was, at the time, the defeated club's worst ever at home. It has since been superseded by the FA Cup defeat at home to Sheffield Wednesday in February 1961, when following a 1-1 draw at Hillsborough, the Owls won 7-2 at Old Trafford. All six of the Forest goals were scored by West and Morris.

Manchester United's poor run of form continued the following weekend when they lost 3-0 at Sunderland, whose side contained Albert Milton at left-back. Teammate Charlie Buchan described Milton as 'five foot six and a half inches of solid manhood, with thighs like tree trunks and the courage of a Lion. He was a grand player and a staunch colleague.'

On the outbreak of hostilities, Milton worked in a munitions factory, turning out for Sunderland Rovers when available. In 1915, he was called up to the Royal Field Artillery (attached to the Durham Light Infantry) and made his way to Flanders to fight in the slaughter of Passchendaele. The day before the main attack, 11 October 1917, Bombardier 151944 Milton was killed in action, aged just thirty-one.

He is commemorated on the Tyne Cot Memorial, one of four to the missing in Belgian Flanders, which cover the area known as the Ypres Salient, maintained in perpetuity by the Commonwealth Graves Commission.

An irony to the tragic death of Milton is that he probably fought within a few miles of his former teammate at Sunderland, Charlie Buchan, who survived all three of the Ypres bloodbaths.

Courageous as a lion, the mud and barbarity of Ypres took Milton's life, like so many others during the First World War.

15

As Title Hopes Fade, a New Era and Ground Beckon

United beat Middlesbrough 2-1 away on 18 December, then lost twice in three days over Christmas 1909 to Sheffield Wednesday. The home fixture on Christmas Day was Roberts' benefit match, and the attendance and receipts meant the £500 he was promised was easily met. Roberts had hoped that his benefit match would have been against Manchester City, but the Citizens' relegation at the end of the previous season ended such hopes; the United captain would have made more from a game against City.

Wednesday won 3-0 at Bank Street and their margin of success was equalled in a 4-1 victory back home when only a great display by Moger kept the score line below that of the earlier United match with Forest. The poor form of both Turnbulls had seen both men left out of the side, and they were replaced by Picken and debutant Ted Connor upfront.

The defeated side did, however, start 1910 in good form but after beating Bradford City 2-0 away on 1 January and drawing 1-1 at Bury, there was disappointment when Burnley gained revenge for the previous season's defeat at home to Manchester United in the FA Cup by beating their conquerors 2-0 at Turf Moor in the first round of the 1910 competition. A crowd of 16,628 saw the Burnley veteran Walter Abbott give his side an early lead, which Smethams added to late in the game as the Cup holders pressed for an equalising goal.

In 1910, Britain was gripped by election fever. The Liberal Party had chosen to seek re-election after their 1909 People's Budget proposals were passed in the House of Commons but rejected by a House of Lords dominated by the large landowners of the Conservative-Unionist opposition.

David Lloyd George, the Chancellor of the Exchequer in the Liberal Government of Herbert Asquith elected in 1906, was determined to 'lift the shadow of the workhouse from the homes of the poor' and believed the best way of doing this was to guarantee an income to people too old to work. In 1908, he introduced the Old Age Pensions Act to provide between 1s (5p) and 5s (25p) to anyone over seventy.

However, paying for these measures would require government revenues to be raised by an additional £16 million, which Lloyd George proposed to collect by increasing income tax on those earning over £3,000 (around £225,000 in current prices) to 1s and 2d (6p) in the pound with a further 'supertax' of 6d (2.5p) for those earning £5,000 a year. With an increase also proposed on inheritance tax and plans for the introduction of a land tax, the proposed budget was opposed by the Conservative and Unionist Party.

The Liberals, with Winston Churchill heading the campaign, responded by making their proposals to reduce the power of the Lords the main issue at the January 1910 general election. Although the Unionists gained more votes, the Liberals maintained power by establishing a coalition with Labour and the Irish Nationalists, and after dropping the land tax proposal, the proposed Budget was subsequently accepted by the Lords.

Despite this, contention between the Government and Lords continued until the second general election was called in December 1910. This again resulted in a hung parliament, with the Liberals continuing to rely on smaller coalition parties to remain in Government and with whom they combined to pass the Parliament Act of 1911 that asserted the supremacy of the House of Commons over the House of Lords.

The whole affair also impacted on one of the great constitutional questions of the period – the struggle in Ireland for Home Rule. The separate Kingdoms of Great Britain and Ireland had merged on 1 January 1801, and over the following years Irish opposition to the Union was strong. By 1870, the Home Rule League sought to achieve a modest form of self-government for Ireland while remaining part of the United Kingdom.

After the December 1910 general election, the nationalist Irish Parliamentary Party, led by John Redmond, saw its chance to achieve Home Rule, agreeing to support the Liberal Party in return for Asquith introducing a Home Rule Bill, and the third such bill was introduced on 11 April 1912 – although it was not to be until May 1914 that it was to finally make it through the Commons.

In six of the nine counties that constitute the historical area known as Ulster, there was considerably less support for Home Rule than in the rest of Ireland. The numerically much larger Protestant community had no wish to share power with what it saw as its inferior Catholic neighbours, and they wished to retain the link with Britain, especially in light of the fact that much of the highly profitable industrial enterprises that provided work were based on the link with the British Empire.

In January 1913, the unionists established the Ulster Volunteer Force with over 100,000 members determined to physically resist the Act's implementation by force of arms. Fully expecting that the British Army would be used to impose 'Dublin' or 'Rome Rule', the UVF imported thousands of rifles from Germany.

Meanwhile, on New Year's Day 1913, their leader, MP Sir Edward Carson, moved an amendment in the Commons to exclude all nine counties of Ulster from the Home Rule Bill. This attempt at partition was vigorously opposed by Nationalists, who themselves began to take up arms for what seemed the inevitable Irish civil war. In the event, the outbreak of larger hostilities across Europe in 1914 led to the suspension of the Act, temporarily postponing the division of Ireland into north and south.

There had been hopes that the match with Tottenham Hotspur on 22 January 1910 would have been the first to be played at Old Trafford. The poor Cup result combined with bad weather meant Bank Street had only 5,000 or 7,000 (the statistics vary) in attendance for its final game of football.

Those fans who did bother to turn up saw their side win 5-0. Spurs lost Percy Humphreys early on, and without their leader the away side crumbled after making a bright start in which Moger had twice saved smartly. Humphreys had been signed from Chelsea in December 1909, and he was to score a vital winning goal against his old club on the final day of the 1909/10 season when the losers of the match were destined to be relegated.

A goal up at half-time, Manchester United quickly trebled their advantage when Roberts, with his first goal of the season, twice ran through the Spurs rearguard before beating John 'Tiny' Joyce. The Spurs 'keeper had joined the club from Millwall – where he was very highly regarded – in November 1909, and was to make 113 appearances for the North Londoners. He was a big, strapping man and surprisingly agile for his size. He remains the only Spurs 'keeper to score in a League match when he netted from the penalty spot against Bolton Wanderers on 10 April 1914. He repeated the feat a month later during a tour match against Bayern Munich.

Late goals from Connor and Meredith – his first in nearly two years – was a fitting send-off to a ground that had little to recommend it aesthetically, but which had been the base for United's first League and FA Cup successes.

There was then a defeat by a goal to nil at Deepdale before Manchester United travelled up to St James' Park and won 4-3 in a seven goal thriller. The away side were a sorry lot at half-time and were losing 3-0 before goals from Roberts and Turnbull made it 3-2. Blott, in his finest game for United, then made it 3-3 before Sandy Turnbull won the game after Moger saved a Bill McCracken penalty.

Belfast-born Bill McCracken was one of the most loathed footballers of his generation. This was as a result of his mastery of the offside trap, which, when it was introduced in 1866, meant a player could be offside if there were fewer than three players between him and the opposing goal line when the ball was played.

Full-back McCracken, one of the game's thinkers, realised that a more effective way of stopping attacks than dispossessing the forwards was to move craftily upfield at opportune times and catch them offside. McCracken so organised his defence that forwards were regularly caught offside. Although his tactics were seen as effective, they were also viewed as unsporting and angered many opposing players and spectators. Herbert Morley, at those other Magpies, Notts County, was also noted for his use of similar tactics.

The rules were changed in 1925, two years after McCracken retired at the end of a nineteen-year playing career with Newcastle in which he collected three League and one FA Cup winners' medals. McCracken also represented Ireland and, following the partition of the country in 1921, Northern Ireland on fifteen occasions, scoring a single goal.

It was probably the away side's best performance of the season and set them up for the first-ever League match at the magnificent new ground, Old Trafford.

Although United were in eighth place in the table, they were only six points behind leaders Aston Villa and the pair would meet each other the week after the Liverpool game.

Bank Street was Manchester United's second ground on which it was possible to charge spectators an entry fee that could then be utilised to improve facilities and, from 1886, pay wages for professional players. The first, North Road (later Northampton Road), was close to the railway yard of Lancashire and Yorkshire Railway, the founders of Newton Heath Lancashire and Railway Cricket and Football Club in 1878. With no changing rooms on the ground, a drainage system that was regularly overwhelmed when it rained and little covered accommodation, facilities were never good. Then when the sponsoring railway company ended its financial support, a decision to look for other, better facilities was taken and Newton Heath moved to Bank Street, Clayton, in 1893, which was three miles from North Road.

The decision to transfer from Bank Street to Old Trafford was the logical conclusion of the decision by five local businessman, including John Henry Davies, to take over Newton Heath's debts of £2,670 in early 1902, and attempt to turn the club into one of the giants of football. First there was the replacement of secretary-manager Jim West by Ernest Mangnall in 1903, followed by giving the new man resources to ensure a promotion bid. There was disappointment when there were third place finishes in 1903/04 and 1904/05. But boosted by the arrival from Bury of Charlie Sagar, whose career was to be cut short by injury, Manchester United won promotion behind Bristol City in 1905/06.

There were plenty of rumours in the 1906/07 season about a proposed move, but it appears that the actual announcement itself came either just before or at the infamous match with Notts County (pp. 71–73) on 11 April 1908. There are likely to have been a number of fans who would not have welcomed the announcement that the club was going to move across Manchester. Few clubs of the size of Manchester United moved grounds in the first decade – technically it was the second – of the twentieth century, with Sunderland moving to Roker Park, Sheffield Wednesday to Hillsborough and Aston Villa to Villa Park in the 1890s.

To some extent then, this was Manchester United catching up with – and overtaking - the other great clubs at the time. Not until Arsenal moved from Plumstead to Highbury in 1913 was another great club to up sticks and move. After Arsenal, the next big club to move was Manchester City in 1924, when they transferred from Hyde Road to Maine Road.

At the time of Manchester United's birth in 1878, the population of Greater Manchester stood at just under 1.8 million, and it was to reach 2.6 million by 1911. Newton Heath had averaged 7,280 at Bank Street in 1893/94 – the fifth highest in the land – and in 1906/07, averaged 20,695, the fourth highest behind Newcastle United, Aston Villa and Manchester City.

The intended new venue was within walking distance of Old Trafford Cricket Ground, home of Lancashire County Cricket Club since 1864. In 1898, Lancashire made the bold decision to buy the ground and some adjoining land, including the Gun Club, from the de Trafford owners for £24,732. It was a big step, but one that in later years was to secure the prosperity and future of the club. The same was to prove true for the football club that became neighbours.

Jimmy Catton, who wrote under the name of Tityrus (a cross between a goat and a sheep designed to symbolise one in authority who leads with strength), was arguably the most important football journalist of the early professional era. When he was appointed editor of the Manchester-based *Athletic News,* he turned it into the most popular football paper in the country. Catton was just 4 feet 10 inches and considered the finest side he ever saw play to be the Preston North End side that did the League and Cup double in the first season of League Football, 1888/89.

On 8 March 1909, he told his readers: 'The west of Manchester is destined to be the Mecca of sportsmen of that great commercial city ... Already we have the Lancashire County Cricket ground, the polo ground, the curling pond, the Manchester Gun club and numerous other organisations of similar character, devoted to pastime and recreation to the west of the city.'

Predicting that the new ground would be opened in September 1909 – the start of the new season – he remarked that 'the contrast between Clayton and the new headquarters of this great football club need not be insisted upon', before going on to remark how Clayton was dominated by about forty massive stacks of belching chimneys. Whereas the football club may remind nearby residents that amusement can be found in a healthy, vigorous manner, he felt that it was only right that an ambitious club should look to locate to a more attractive location.

The new venue was to be between the Cheshire Lines railway and the Bridgewater Canal, close to the Chester Road in Stretford. Catton predicted there would not be any problems reaching the new venue, as electric tramcars already ran from Clayton to Old Trafford while it was proposed to lay down a circular tramway siding just off Chester Road.

There would be further expansion with the Cheshire Lines railway company intending to open a special station within easy walking distance of the new ground. This would not contain a running or cycling track around the pitch, but would be solely dedicated to football.

Up to 100,000 spectators, with 12,000 seated, could expect to be accommodated, ensuring that some of the greatest matches could be brought to Manchester. England, internationally, at this time did not have a regular ground and were not to have one until Wembley opened in 1923. The Crystal Palace, the FA Cup final venue at the beginning of the twentieth century, had a poor viewing reputation. It was intended that Old Trafford would have a good reputation, with Catton telling readers,

> The ground will be rectangle in shape with the corners rounded and it is designed so that everybody will be excavated to a depth of nine feet from the ground level so that the boundary or containing wall which is to surround the whole place will only be thirty feet high.

One hundred steps of terracing were to be constructed with 'of course Leitch's patient crush barriers'. Archibald Leitch of Manchester was the only designer employed by Manchester United, and Catton waxed lyrical about how the Glaswegian – whose previous work included the likes of Tottenham, Rangers, Hampden Park, Everton, Fulham, Chelsea and Sunderland – was planning to construct easy stairs for whichever entrance spectators used to reach the seats or terracing.

Most grounds at this time had a paddock in front of the grandstand seats. This was not going to be the case at Old Trafford, where the seats would run directly back to the stand. There would be fifty tiers of seats, but there would be stairs up to the loftiest sections so as to ensure spectators seated high up had no need to disturb those lower down when taking their seats. It was a principle that Leitch was keen to keep throughout the new ground. Underneath the grandstand there would be a corridor with tea rooms, referee apartments, players' facilities, a gym, billiard room and laundry.

The ground would occupy 16 acres and have an outward circumference of approximately 2,000 feet. Catton stated,

> This is a palatial ground which will challenge comparison with any in Great Britain. The executives of the club are to be congratulated on their spirited policy which [will] no doubt be met with reward from the football public.

Nevertheless, these executives – particularly club secretary J. J. Bentley (who wrote for the *Athletic News'* great rival the *Cricket and Football Field*) – suggested omitting the cover on the terracing opposite the grandstand and reducing the height of the terracing. A cycling track was to be built round the pitch. These changes cut the capacity of the ground to an anticipated 80,000 and also reduced the overall project costs to £60,000 – still double the initial figure reported for the new ground.

Attempts by Leitch to persuade the Cheshire Lines Railway to loan £10,000 were to prove ultimately unproductive. This was despite the fact that the company was certain to benefit if Manchester United were successful on the field, as this would lead to many more people using their facilities to get to the match. The ground was to be a Manchester United Football Club venture only, and this may explain why builder Humphreys of Knightsbridge had to constantly badger the club to ensure they were paid. Other local traders faced similar problems, and there can be little doubt that the venture must have caused some sleepless nights for John Davies and his fellow directors, especially when they were threatened with legal action by contractors worried about unpaid bills for work already completed. In the event, missing the planned opening date of 22 January 1910 for the game against Tottenham Hotspur must have been the least of the club's worries.

Daily Sketch, Thursday 17 February 1910

> Manchester United's new ground at Old Trafford is going to be a real beauty ... and when it is finished it will be the finest in Great Britain ... the huge grandstand, which stretches right along one side, is unlike anything I have ever seen. All the occupants will be well protected from the weather ... The humble-spectator – the man who

can afford no more than a 'tanner' for his afternoon's sport – has also
been well catered for. He has not been provided with, and cannot
expect, any overhead covering but he can keep his feet dry for he will
be accommodated on a series of cemented terraces, any one of which
will give him an uninterrupted view of the game.

The decision not to provide covering did, of course, save money but
in an era when catching a cold really could be death of you – in 1918
the flu pandemic that swept across the world caused the deaths of at
least 50 million – it was likely to reduce the size of the attendance on
rainy days of which, of course, Manchester is famous.

Entrance fees to the new ground were fixed at 6*d* (2.5p) for the
ground, and from one to two shillings (5–10p) for the covered
stand, while reserved seats in the centre of the grandstand were 5*s*
(25p) These seats proved to be plush tip-up affairs.

Local businesses were hoping to cash in on the increased number
of visitors to the area, and Mr J. H. Hargreaves, owner of the
nearby Dog and Partridge Hotel, attempted to obtain a licence to
sell alcohol at the ground. He wanted to sell in five bars from half
an hour before kick-off at 3.30 p.m. until 6.00 p.m.

The applications was refused by a stipendiary magistrate – Mr
J. M. Yates, KC – on the grounds that such applications needed
to go before the council meeting of licensing authorities. Yates felt
'the football public must be a curious lot, if they cannot watch for
two hours without having a drink'. The decision must have come
as a blow not only to a thirsty watching public – many of whom
would have arrived at the ground only a short time after finishing
work – but to Manchester United, for it would have dealt a blow
to anticipated future receipts. Even on a gate of over 40,000, match
day receipts were just £500 and so it was going to take some time
to recoup the outlay of £60,000.

The temperance movement, which urged people to avoid alcohol
or drink only in moderation, would no doubt have approved of
Mr Yates' actions. This has been a significant mass movement until
relatively recent times and even in 1922, it still had sufficient punch
to land a blow on Winston Churchill when the Scottish Prohibition
Party beat him – and every other candidate – to win the Dundee
seat in that year's general election. During the First World War, pub
hours were limited, beer was watered down and it was subjected
to a penny (0.5p) a pint extra tax. Manchester City's Maine Road

was originally known as Dog Kennel Lane, but had its name changed when its owners, the Temperance Movement, successfully petitioned Manchester Corporation during the 1870s.

In the days leading up to the opening game, there was frantic building activity with the *Manchester Evening News* reporting, on Valentine's Day, that there could be found

> a staff of between three and four hundred men hard at work; and by Saturday next, when the ground will be opened, accommodation will be found for 60,000 people. The biggest task before the officials at present is that of preparing the entrance to the ground, but this work is being carried on most expeditiously, and by noon on Saturday intending spectators will find nothing to complain about. The entrance to Warwick Road North, at the end of which their ground is situated, is being widened, and with the exception of the narrow bridge which spans the railway there should be ample space for the crowd.
>
> On the huge covered stand itself painters, plumbers, carpenters, and a variety of workmen are busily occupied, and quite a large staff is engaged fixing the "tip-up" chairs and laying linoleum on the reserved portion of the structure. Trains will be run to the cricket ground station, which is about five minutes from the ground, and there is some talk of a service of motor 'buses' from Trafford Park Station to the ground. The playing pitch looks in ideal condition and given a fine day there should be a capital game played in the presence of a record crowd for the Manchester district.

The large number of workers at Old Trafford in the days leading up to its opening had to contend with a fierce gale on the Thursday morning. The *Manchester Evening News* reported that a number of people had been injured and the grandstand at Bank Street had been blown down.

Manchester United Ground Damaged

> Grand stand blown down at Clayton
> Shortly after noon today the wind caused great damage on the old ground of Manchester United club at Clayton, the grand-stand in Bank Street being almost swept away. The roof was blown down in the street, finally alighting upon a row of houses opposite. The hoarding

at the back of the stand was blown out, and as showing the terrific force of the wind it may be stated that the brick foundation of the stand was displaced. Some parts of the stand roof were blown into the next street, and broke several windows. Luckily, no one was injured. In one house a large piece of wood crashed through the window of an upstairs front room and badly damaged a dressing stand.

Was Old Trafford a White Elephant?

There is little doubt that in the long run, the decision to up sticks and move to Old Trafford proved the right one for Manchester United. That certainly was not the case, though, for almost forty years. Then Matt Busby arrived at the club. Soon after, United was able to take advantage of over £22,000 in compensation from the War Damage Commission to replace what had become a dilapidated stadium, even before the Luftwaffe bombed most parts of it to the floor during the Second World War.

Manchester United's gates in 1908/09 averaged 18,150 and rose to just 24,190 in 1910/11. Such a massive ground was rarely full over the next three decades, and only on three occasions did the club average more than 30,000 a match during the season. Between 1929 and 1932, the average gate was only just over 14,000. It must have been hard for players to motivate themselves when there were so few people in such a massive arena. Whereas the FA chose to take the 1910 FA Cup semi, the 1911 FA Cup final replay and the 1915 Final to Old Trafford, the ground staged just seven more semi-finals in the following forty-four seasons of Cup football.

The period following the end of the 1910/11 season was to be followed by a lengthy barren spell in which the peak of Manchester United's achievement was an unsuccessful place in the semi-final of 1925/26 season. It could well have been that at least some of the funds that were found to build Old Trafford could have been used to retain Charlie Roberts and Alec Bell in 1913. Funds could have also been used to recruit some of the finest talent in the land. For example, in 1911, Blackburn Rovers spent £1,809 on Jock Simpson from Falkirk and two years later, spent £2,000 on West Ham's Danny Shea and in March 1921, Huddersfield Town recruited Clem Stephenson for £3,000 from Aston Villa. With a fading side, Manchester United almost went bust due to their low attendances in the two decades that followed the end of the First World War.

Opening Old Trafford Match on 19 February 1910

Manchester United 3 (Homer, S. Turnbull, Wall), Liverpool 4 (Goddard 2, Stewart 2).
Man Utd: Moger, Stacey, Hayes, Duckworth, Roberts, Blott, Meredith, Halse, Homer, S. Turnbull, Wall.
Liverpool: Hardy, Chorlton, Rogers, Robinson, Harrop, Bradley, Goddard, Stewart, Parkinson, Orr, McDonald.
Referee: A. McArthur (Newcastle).

Liverpool had never managed to win at Bank Street, losing five and drawing twice. Liverpool were backed, though, by a considerable number of their own followers, who poured off the trains from Merseyside. After half an hour of the game, many must have wished they had stayed at home. Yes, it was great to see this fabulous new arena, but United were 2-0 up.

Old Trafford's first goal was worthy of the occasion, Duckworth's free-kick dropped over the Liverpool defence where Sandy Turnbull hurled himself headlong, just a foot off the ground, to head it past the Liverpool 'keeper. The hundreds of home fans who had brought bells with them and who were wearing red-and-white suits were overjoyed. The second came when Hardy saved Halse's powerful shot but was helpless to prevent Tom Homer netting the rebound.

It was Arthur Goddard who reduced the arrears early in the second half, after a fine flowing Liverpool move left him in the clear. However, this looked to be a mere consolation when Wall, in trademark fashion, cut in from the left to hit the ball across the goal and into the net to make it 3-1. After that, however, Liverpool were clearly the better side. Goddard made it 3-2, then Stewart got his second of the season against Manchester United to make it 3-3. Moments later, he got his third and Liverpool's fourth of this particular game and from 3-1 down Liverpool had come back to win away at Manchester United for the first time ever in a 4-3 thriller.

The home side would have to wait until they beat Sheffield United 1-0 in the next home game for a first victory at their new ground. Yet just to show they really did like the place, they went on to win the remaining six homes games of the season. In fact, they were to only lose once at home over the next eighteen months. Old Trafford from the very start had become a fortress.

16

LATE SEASON SLUMP

If United were to have even the slightest chance of winning the title in 1910, then success was vital in the game at Villa Park on 26 February 1910. With Wall and Hayes selected to play in the Inter-league match with the Scottish League, there were chances for Connor and Holden in the away XI, who were 4-1 down at the interval with Joe Walters having taken advantage of an injury to Roberts by scoring three times. Three further second half goals meant Villa won 7-1, and it was a sorry defeated side that left the pitch at the conclusion. The result remains Manchester United's record defeat, and it could have been many more if Moger had not played pretty well. Villa were now eight points ahead of Mangnall's side and also had a game in hand.

A first Old Trafford success – 1-0 against Sheffield United – followed by a 0-0 draw at Arsenal was quickly followed by two further home successes, this time against Bolton Wanderers and Bristol City. Five goals were notched against Wanderers, who failed to reply, with all five forwards – Meredith, Halse, James Turnbull, Picken and Wall – scoring. Despite these results, United remained off the pace and were nine points behind leaders Villa with just a dozen matches remaining. The gap became even bigger when only one point was won in the Easter away games to Chelsea and Bristol City.

Having invested so heavily in the new ground, a crowd of just 5,500 for the fixture on Wednesday 6 April 1910 against Everton must have been a real concern for the United directors. The home side won 3-2 and, as a result, the Toffees became the first side to lose twice at Old Trafford, as on 31 March 1910 they had been beaten 3-0 by Second Division Barnsley in an FA Cup semi-final replay. This marked the first occasion when Old Trafford hosted prestigious matches involving sides other than Manchester United and the share of the revenue that the hosts would have received from a 55,000-strong crowd must have been a big boost to the coffers. Defeat in the FA Cup had also come at a heavy cost for Everton, whose captain Jack Taylor was struck so heavily by the ball in his larynx that he felt compelled to retire from the game after 15 minutes – he never played competitive football again. Barnsley thus qualified to play Newcastle United in the final to see who would replace Manchester United as FA Cup holders.

Manchester United were to finish the season by winning two, drawing one and losing one of their remaining four games. The final match of the season saw Picken score all his side's goals in a 4-1 defeat of Middlesbrough at Old Trafford. The 1908 League champions finished the 1910 season in fifth place, eight points behind the champions, Aston Villa, who recorded their fifth top flight success.

1909/10 Record
All home games up to and including Tottenham Hotspur at Bank Street. All home games from Liverpool onwards at Old Trafford.

September
Bradford City [H] 1-0
Bury [H] 2-0
Notts County [H] 2-1
Tottenham Hotspur [A] 2-2
Preston North End [H] 1-1
Notts County [A] 2-3

October
Newcastle United [H] 1-1
Liverpool [A] 2-3
Aston Villa [H] 2-0
Sheffield United [A] 1-0
Arsenal [H] 1-0

November
Bolton Wanderers [A] 3-2
Chelsea [H] 2-0
Blackburn Rovers [A] 2-3
Nottingham Forest [H] 2-6

December
Sunderland [A] 0-3
Middlesbrough [A] 2-1
Sheffield Wednesday [H] 0-3
Sheffield Wednesday [A] 1-4

January
Bradford City [A] 2-0
Bury [A] 1-1
Burnley [A] FA Cup 0-2
Tottenham Hotspur [H] 5-0

February
Preston North End [A] 0-1
Newcastle United [A] 4-3
Liverpool [H] 3-4
Aston Villa [A] 1-7

March
Sheffield United [H] 1-0
Arsenal [A] 0-0
Bolton Wanderers [H] 5-0
Bristol City [H] 2-1
Chelsea [A] 1-1
Bristol City [A] 1-2

April
Blackburn Rovers [H] 2-1
Everton [H] 3-2
Nottingham Forest [A] 0-2
Sunderland [H] 2-0
Everton [A] 3-3
Middlesbrough [H] 4-1

Manchester United finished the season in fifth place with forty-five points, eight points behind champions Aston Villa, and with a home record of 14-2-3, having scored 41 goals and conceded 20. Away from home the record was 5-5-9 with 28 goals scored and 41 conceded.

The following were signed to play for Manchester United in 1909/10:

Sam Blott signed for Manchester United in the summer of 1909. He was to go on and make nineteen first team League appearances in which he scored twice, of which the most important was the third at St James' Park in February 1910, a game in which Manchester United recovered from being three down to win 4-3. Blott's son, Cyril, followed his example and played for Charlton Athletic between 1937 and 1939, before joining the Army, eventually reaching the rank of Major.

Arthur Whalley signed for Manchester United from Blackpool in June 1909. The fee was just £90, and although he had made only five appearances for the Seasiders, the money proved a wise investment as he went on to make 106 appearances in which he scored six goals from half-back. He made fifteen appearances in 1910/11, and this qualified him for a League championship medal. Badly injured in 1913/14, he played just once the following season before enlisting in the Army and being seriously injured in the Battle of Third Ypres (Passchendaele) in 1917. He made a full recovery and appeared in twenty-three League matches in 1919/20, but when United's board refused to offer him a benefit match he joined Southend United in September 1920.

Ted Connor was to make fifteen appearances for Manchester United in the 1909/10 and 1910/11 seasons. The winger, though, failed to displace either Billy Meredith or George Wall and in June 1911, Sheffield United paid £750 to sign him. Connor later scouted for United and was an office worker at Old Trafford for many years.

Tony Donnelly signed for Manchester United at the start of the 1908/09 season and was to go on and make thirty-seven first-team appearances at full-back. He won a League championship medal by making fifteen League appearances in 1910/11. He joined Glentoran in the summer of 1913.

Appearances in 1909/10

	League	FA Cup
Moger	36	1
Stacey	32	1

Wall	32	1
Meredith	31	1
Hayes	30	1
Duckworth	29	1
Roberts	28	1
Halse	29	1
Bell	27	-
A. Turnbull	26	1
Picken	19	1
J. Turnbull	19	-
Homer	17	-
Livingstone	16	-
Blott	10	-
Whalley	9	-
Connor	8	-
Holden	7	-
Donnelly	4	-
Downie	3	-
Hooper	2	-
Round	2	-
Bannister	1	-
Burgess	1	-
Curry	-	1
Ford	1	-
Quinn	1	-

Scorers

Wall	14
A. Turnbull	13
J. Turnbull	9
Homer	8
Picken	7
Halse	6
Meredith	5
Roberts	4
Blott	1
Connor	1
Hooper	1

17

NEW MAN PROVES BIG SUCCESS

The 1910/11 season opened on Thursday 1 September when a crowd approaching 15,000 were at the Manor Field, Woolwich, to see Arsenal take on Manchester United, for whom there was a debut for Enoch West, the Nottingham Forest player who had finished as top scorer in First Division in 1907/08.

The highlight of the game was the battle between Andy Ducat – as well as playing international football, he was also a cricketer of some distinction who played once for England and is the only person to have died while batting at Lord's – and George Wall out on the United left. The contest was won by the latter with an impressive display that constantly forced the Arsenal side on to the defensive. West also showed he was going to be a positive addition to his new side. The former Forest man capped a fine performance by scoring the winner, after Arsenal had responded to Halse's opening goal through debutant Willis Rippon, one of only two goals the player scored for the Gunners. West's ability to hold up the ball and distribute to his fellow forwards was matched by his disposition to forage for his own opportunities, while for Arsenal fans there was pleasure in seeing Sands back in the side after a long injury, and new signing Alf Common made a number of important touches. Common had left Middlesbrough after he was offered a free by the cash-strapped Teesside club if he did not claim the £250 benefit they had promised him.

The first home game of the season took place just two days later, when the visitors were Blackburn Rovers. The United's programme – Vol. 1 – cost one penny and the front cover contained an advert on where to dine and how to get there. Only by opening the inside pages would you discover United's opponents. Modern-day programmes contain many words but are rarely as blunt as the club's comments were for the opening paragraph of the sixteen-page programme.

> Whatever fate may have in store for the United team this season, the management, at least, is free from reproach of having neglected to strengthen the side where an appearance of weakness had manifested itself ... those conversant with the varying fortunes of the game have nothing but recommendation for the promptness shown in repairing the defection of James Turnbull [who returned to Scotland without agreement on terms for a fourth season and later signed for Bradford City]. Although I did not consider the Scotsman an ideal centre-forward by any means; it is somewhat of a tribute to the esteem in which he was held in other quarters that he is replaced by one of the best pivots in the country. Possessing all of the physical attributes of his predecessor, whose thrust-fulness he recalls, West displays a cleverness of footwork to which Jas Turnbull was a stranger...

It also noted that the United executive had signed Hofton from Glossop because of the 'uncertainty respecting the complete return to form of Dick Holden'. Hofton himself had required an operation, undertaken by Dr Thorburn, before being able to resume training and it was to be a number of weeks into the season before he was fit enough to play for the first team.

The advent of a programme meant it was possible for Manchester United to increase their advertising revenue, and it contained a one-page advert for ale houses serving Groves & Whitnall's beers before and after the game. There were 100,000 pubs in England and Wales, all belonging to the local area where they stood. The pubs dispensed a huge variety of local brews – mostly flat, dark brown and warm – and were frequented almost exclusively by men. Women who entered them were usually forced to sit in the snug bar at the back.

The role of women though was changing quickly, and the period following Queen Victoria's death in 1901 was marked by the emergence of the Women's Social and Political Union, dedicated to ensuring equal voting rights for women. Many women went to prison for a cause that was ultimately successful. At the same time, the radical change in the economic role of married women in particular was still on the horizon, with only 10 per cent having a recognised occupation and most women who married still quit work in 1911, as their husbands were against them going out to work and believed a family wage was the way to earn respectability as well as keeping wages high.

None of this made women's lives easy, especially when an average of six children came along, as many lived in damp, dark overcrowded tenements infested with bugs. With just a £1 a week – and from which 7s (35p) was needed to pay the rent – to feed, heat and clothe six children and two adults, a wife then had to master a limited budget and was constantly asking for help from neighbours or credit from the grocers. Taking in washing was another method of supplementing income and there was also the pawn shop when things got really tough. Many women often deprived themselves of food in order to ensure their husband and working children were properly fed in order for them to be able to withstand the rigours of manual work.

There was an advert in the programme for Oxo, which secretary/manager Ernest Mangnall helped promote by saying: 'Our trainer finds OXO most suitable for keeping the players fit.' There were adverts for Alec Watson's – sports outfitters to Manchester United AFC – and a full-page advert for Tyldesley and Holbrook sports in which the 'World Famous VICTOR Footballs for both Association or Rugby' were prominent, along with football boots costing from 4s 11d (24.5p) up to 10s 6d (52.5p)

The line-up for both sides was listed with Ashcroft in goal for the away side at No. 1 and Moger in the Manchester United goal at No. 22. West was listed at No. 14 and Roberts at centre-half was No. 18. Not that any players had numbers on their backs at this time, and it was not until the 1920s that the game began to experiment with the idea. The first major game when numbers were added to shirts was for the 1933 FA Cup final between Everton and Manchester City. The former wore 1–11 and the latter 12–22. The numbers 1–11 on each side became standard a few years later.

The new United programme informed its readers that 'any changes in the teams will be notified by number on the board which will be sent round the enclosure'.

When the game with Blackburn started there was a rare mistake by away captain Crompton, when he misjudged the ball in the swirling wind and the ever-alert Turnbull took swift advantage to drive his side ahead on 3 minutes. The goal of the game – and possibly the whole season – was the second home goal in an eventual 3-2 success.

Following some fine interchanging of passes and positions between Meredith and Halse, the latter confronted Bradshaw before back heeling the ball for West to crash it home. It was Meredith who scored the third goal for United with Rovers' efforts coming from Davies and Eddie Latheron. Having lost their first League match at Old Trafford, Manchester United had won the next eight. Rovers were to finish the season down in twelfth place, and there was little to think that they would go on to win the League title twice in the following two seasons. The signing of Jock Simpson – who many placed in the same category as Meredith – from Falkirk helped turn a decent side into a good one.

In 1909/10, Nottingham Forest had only managed to taste success at home in the League on four occasions, which was the worst record in Division One. One of these victories had come late in the season when they had beaten Manchester United 2-0, and by doing so recorded the double for the season after winning 6-1 at Bank Street in November 1909.

Forest continued their impressive form in games between the sides by winning 2-1 at home in the third match of the 1910/11 season. The winner came from Meredith's Welsh international colleague, the brilliant Grenville Morris, who after the diminutive Derrick had equalised Turnbull's early goal, scored with 20 minutes of the match remaining. Try as they might after that, the away side rarely looked like grabbing a point and went down to their first defeat of the season.

The fourth game of the season saw a crowd of 60,000 pack out Old Trafford for the eagerly awaited derby with City. Having lost their entire first team squad in 1906, City appeared to have survived only to be relegated at the end of the 1908/09 season. Promotion though had been won at the first attempt, and the game was to be first of many thrillers between the two Manchester sides played at Old Trafford. City had won one and drawn two of their opening three games.

The match was to end in a victory for the home side, but only because the away side failed to convert a penalty kick. Many more penalties were missed during this period as 'keepers were allowed to advance from their line as the kicker moved to strike the ball.

At the same time, City failed miserably to press home the advantage they had gained from Lyall winning the toss and choosing to make their opponents play into a bright, dazzling sun, which must have made defending especially difficult at corners and free-kicks.

There is a saying that the best form of defence is attack and it was, in fact, Manchester United who started the game on the offensive and Lyall in the City goal was called upon to clear on many occasions. With hardly any wind, the shirt-sleeved crowd was left thrilled when Meredith made a marvellous dribbling run before finishing with a shot that whistled just over. How City fans must have wished he was still playing for their team, especially when they enjoyed a decent share of possession in the first period. Indeed, Stacey was very fortunate to escape punishment for a series of rough challenges on Joe Dorsett.

The game's opening goal came after Lyall did superbly to keep out a powerful drive from Duckworth, but when the ball spun free West pushed it into the net accompanied by the enormous cheers of the United faithful. Within less than a minute, they had even more to cheer when Sandy Turnbull got beyond the City defence to knock home Meredith's acute angled pass and make it 2-0. The away side were given an opportunity to get back into the match shortly afterwards, when Linkson handled in the penalty area. Moger, however, saved Lol Jones' first effort and then repelled the City players' second effort, all to the accompaniment of a roar that could probably be heard a mile away. The interval thus arrived with United leading City 2-0.

On the restart, the sun had dropped and United pushed forward in search of a third, Wall tested Lyall with a shot that the City custodian dealt with confidently. Then, on 58 minutes, Linkson miskicked and Jones atoned for his penalty miss by scoring to reduce the arrears. Jones should have levelled only to fire wide from close-in.

There was some good fortune for the losing side when United twice hit the woodwork, but it mattered little in the end as United held on to win 2-1. The result raised the victors to third in the table, two points behind Sunderland.

The bright opening to the season by Ernest Mangnall's side continued over the next four matches, all of which were won. The first was at Goodison Park and although there was only a single goal, the game was an exciting one in which the away side's defence played remarkably well given the pressure piled on them by the home forwards. At the same time, Everton did miss a number of good chances that would have earned them at least a point.

The game was played at a fast pace throughout and two half-backs stood out as the best players on the day – Makepeace for Everton and Roberts for Manchester United. Very often these players snuffed out a shooting opportunity for their opponents and also had the skill to find their own players when they were under pressure in possession of the ball. As captain, Roberts also was seen constantly urging his teammates to greater efforts, it was one of his finest performances during his time at Manchester United. The only goal came when Sandy Turnbull received the ball from West and then turned to send it high out of the reach of Scott and into the net. It was a great goal and worthy of winning any game.

The performance by the winning side was heart-warming for the travelling fans, who had seen their side perform heroically. There was also a special mention for Meredith in the *Liverpool Courier* on the Monday following the game, when the paper's reporter commented, 'Meredith wears well, and when he gets an opening he is exceedingly difficult to stop. He is yet a football "star" and likely to remain so for some time.'

After beating Sheffield Wednesday 3-2 at Old Trafford, Manchester United moved alongside Sunderland at the top of the table with ten points from twelve. It was another fine match in which West equalised Robertson's opening goal. Wall scored twice in the second half and played brilliantly. It was a return to form for Wall, made especially notable as his partner, Sandy Turnbull, was injured early on.

The game at Ashton Gate drew a crowd of 20,000. Billy Wedlock had been granted the game as his benefit match, but the size of the crowd meant he would only receive £200, a meagre return for his many years of efforts in what was Bristol City's most successful period, during which he made over 400 first-team appearances and also played twenty-six times for England. The East Stand at Ashton Gate, where Bristol City moved permanently for the start of the 1904/05 season, is today named in Wedlock's honour.

Roberts, Wedlock's rival for the centre-half position at international level, was at his very best in the game, and despite playing with just ten men after Alec Bell retired injured in the first half, a neat effort from Halse saw both points return north. Back at Old Trafford, the 1910 FA Cup winners, Newcastle United, were defeated 2-0 and the 50,000-strong crowd meant that with receipts of £1,600 both Holden (the captain for the day) and Picken would collect £300 each for a game that had been earmarked for their benefit match. Wind ruined the match, but goals from Halse and a late Sandy Turnbull effort maintained the winning side's good opening to the season.

A 2-2 draw at White Hart Lane maintained the good run, but there was a shock when, having won eleven home matches in a row, United lost 2-1 to Middlesbrough at Old Trafford. The Teessiders arrived unbeaten in the season and won through goals from Pentland and San Call, with Sandy Turnbull replying for the defeated side. The victorious side contained Andy Jackson, another player who was killed during the war.

Preston North End had twice won the League themselves, both in the first two seasons of League football. Unfortunately, no trophy was presented until Everton won the League in 1890/91. North End had been overtaken by more glamorous sides since 1888/89, and Aston Villa – in 1896/97 – had even equalled their League and FA Cup double winning feat. Preston had suffered the indignity of relegation in 1900/01, but bounced back up three seasons later. In 1906, Charlie Parker became secretary-manager at Deepdale and he built his side around centre-half Joseph McCall.

On 5 November 1910, there was little action of any description in a dull first half between Preston and Manchester United. The away side improved slightly in the second, and goals from Turnbull and West were sufficient to record a 2-0 success in a game played before a crowd of 13,500.

Seven days later the game at Old Trafford was perhaps even worse and this time there were no goals as Notts County, courtesy of a great last minute save by Iremonger to deny West, claimed a point.

The local derby with Oldham Athletic, playing their first season of top flight football after winning promotion at the end of the 1909/10 season, was a much more feisty affair, and the 25,000 packed inside Boundary Park witnessed a one-sided game in which Athletic 'keeper Hugh McDonald kept the score line down to 3-1, with United's goals coming from Turnbull (2) and Wall. The latter had struggled in the first part of the season, and many attributed this to the exhausting four-month summer tour he, Duckworth and Hayes, who played just one first team match during the season, had undertaken right across South Africa with the FA.

Turnbull had been cautioned during the match for making a series of remarks to the referee and warned that if he repeated them he would be dismissed. Coming off the pitch at the end of the game, the United forward approached the referee and told him that he had repeated the words but he hadn't heard them.

The winning side moved level with Sunderland at the top of the table, but were beaten the following weekend at Anfield against a struggling Liverpool side. This, plus a heavy fog that prevented spectators from seeing the action at the other end of the pitch, meant the crowd was just 8,000. Those who missed the action were denied a treat.

Sandy Turnbull opened the scoring before Oscar Linkson brought down Parkinson and Arthur Goddard drew the sides level. Fortunately, the fog lifted at the start of the second period and the crowd saw Moger make a tremendous save from Goddard. Liverpool were not going to be denied and Parkinson made it 2-1 after an hour and, with 12 minutes remaining, Jimmy Steward doubled the home advantage. A late Charlie Roberts goal failed to prevent a deserved victory for the Merseysiders and, as is often the case in games between these sides, the form book had been thrown out of the window.

Three days before the game at Anfield, Hawley Harvey Crippen had been hung at Pentonville Prison in one of the most famous murder cases in history. Crippen was an American, born in Michigan in 1862, who qualified as a doctor in 1885 and worked for a patent medicine company. He had come to England in 1900 and lived at No. 39 Hilldrop Crescent, Holloway, with his second wife Cora Turner, who was better known by her stage name of Belle Elmore.

After a party at their home on 31 January 1910, Cora disappeared and shortly afterwards Crippen moved his mistress Ethel le Neve into the house, and she began to wear his wife's clothing and jewellery. Cora Turner's friends reported their suspicions to the police; Crippen had been telling people that she had moved back to the USA to see a sick relative.

Detective Chief Inspector Walter Dew visited Crippen, and left the premises after Crippen had claimed that his wife had eloped with a lover and a search had not revealed anything of a suspicious nature.

However, Dew's visit panicked Crippen and Ethel le Neve and they fled the country for Antwerp, from where they took a cabin on SS *Montrose* bound for Canada. Alerted by their disappearance, Scotland Yard performed another three searches of the house and during the fourth and final one, remains of a human body were discovered beneath the cellar. Dr Bernard Spilsbury, the famous pathologist, identified the body as that of Mrs Crippen from a piece of abdominal scar tissue, and found that there were traces of a poison hyoscine in the body.

The search for Crippen was assisted by the Master of the SS *Montrose* who suspected that the 'boy' accompanying one of his passengers, Mr. Robinson, was Ethel le Neve in disguise. He went down in history as the first to use the telegraph to relay his conclusions to the ship's owners and the police. Walter Dew took a faster ship, the SS *Laurentic*, and arrested Crippen on 31 July before he could land in Canada.

At Crippen's trial, the jury took just 27 minutes to convict him of murder, and he was hanged by John Ellis on 23 November 1910 at Pentonville Prison, London. Ethel le Neve, however, was acquitted. In 1963 a feature film, *Dr Crippen*, was released with Donald Pleasance in the title role.

Oscar Linkson retained his place at right back for the match with Bury at Old Trafford in early December 1910. In 1901, Linkson was just thirteen when his elder brother Sidney died of injuries sustained during the second Boer War of 1899 to 1902. He was one of 29,000 Briton's killed in the war; another 16,000 died of disease.

On leaving school, Oscar became a painter but his display for an amateur football side, the Pirates, had been good enough to attract the attention of Manchester United, and he signed for the club in 1908. Unusually, he chose to remain in London with his family and travel to Manchester and play when selected. The *Athletic News* commented on his play as follows: 'A nicely built lad, nimble on his feet, and kicks well.'

Linkson made a total of fifty-nine first team appearances for Manchester United before signing for Shelbourne in the summer of 1913. Two years later, he was persuaded to sign up with the 1st Football Battalion of the Middlesex Regiment. This had been formed on 12 December 1914, and England international Frank Buckley was the first to enlist. The Battalion suffered heavy losses at the Battles of Delville Wood and Guillemont during the Battle of the Somme, during which more than 1,000,000 men in total were killed or injured. Linkson went missing on 8 August 1916 at Guillemont, a strategic area whose control by the Germans effectively divided allied forces. His body was never recovered and he left behind a wife and two children.

There were only 7,000 inside Old Trafford, and the home fans were disappointed when after racing a two-goal lead courtesy of Homer and Turnbull, their side had been pegged back when Currie scored either side of the interval. The winning goal was hotly contested by the away side after the referee decided that Homer's corner kick had crossed the goal line before being scrambled away by the Bury rearguard. Given a late opportunity to draw level, Bury regretted allowing Hibbert – after Stacey had pushed him – to take the resulting penalty. The striker had failed to net from a similar opportunity the previous weekend and again failed miserably.

Having missed six consecutive matches, there was a return to the starting line-up for Dick Holden when United made the short trip to Bramall Lane. He played poorly though and the away side lost 2-0. The following game at home was against League champions Aston Villa, who arrived having won every one of their matches since October 15. The match saw Tony Donnelly switch from his usual left to right-back position, and he played impressively enough for the *Manchester Courier* to hope that United had found an answer to their problems at that position caused by the loss of Holden. His fellow full-back Stacey combined superbly with Bell to constantly stifle the Villa right pairing of Wallace and Walters.

Moger made two great saves from a Walters and then a Bache header, before Turnbull scored a great goal when he made space and when Wall found him, the ex-Hurlford man beat Arthur Cartlidge with a delightfully placed finish from the corner of the box. West doubled the advantage when he skilfully directed the ball with his head past the Villa 'keeper to give the home side both points in a 2-0 victory that raised hopes of a second title success in four seasons.

Just four days later, on 21 December 1910, 344 men and boys lost their lives at the Pretoria Pit Disaster, Westhoughton. They were working five coal seams of the Manchester coalfield that was mined extensively until the last quarter of the twentieth century. Just two men – Joseph Staveley and William Davenport – survived the gas explosion that killed their workmates. This was the second worst mining accident in England and yet even before the last body was recovered, production resumed on 11 January 1911. Coal was vital as the basic form of energy for this period – steam – and at least 1,000 miners died each year in this period, digging it out of the ground with more than 10 per cent of the labour force injured annually.

Mining in the UK employed 971,000 in 1911, thus making it the third biggest employer after agriculture, with 1.2 million people, and domestic service, at 1.3 million. Britain's better off were kept in comfort by an army of domestic servants, who were paid much less than in other jobs but 'enjoyed' free board and lodging at the expense of working under a strict hierarchical regime.

Wearside also saw its own share of mining disasters in the twentieth century, and there would no doubt have been strong sympathy

among the miners and shipyard workers who packed out Roker Park
on Christmas Eve to see their side face Manchester United in 1911.
Sunderland had last won the title in 1902/03, and fans of the famous
old club had high hopes that 1910/11 would see the League trophy
on display for the fifth time at the end of the season.

The crowd of 24,000 contained many shipyard workers, who at
this time made up around a third of the town's adult population.
Sunderland had been building ships since at least 1346, and by
the start of the twentieth century, cargo ships and tankers were
the main types of vessels created in a town then described as 'the
largest shipbuilding town in the world'. The period 1908–10 saw
a national fall in ship production and Sunderland suffered badly
during these two years.

In 1910/11, Sunderland were unbeaten at home having won six
and drawn three of their nine games at Roker Park, and so it was a
great result by Manchester United to win by two goals to one with
Meredith and Turnbull scoring for the victors, a result that dropped
the defeated side from first to fourth in the table afterwards. The
victory was achieved despite the away side falling behind early on
to a Henry Low goal, and the winner from Meredith came late in
the game when both sides appeared to be willing to accept a point.

Buoyed by this victory on Boxing Day 1910, Manchester United
gave a thrilling display to send Woolwich Arsenal home beaten 5-0
with a pair of goals each from Picken and West, supplemented by
one from Meredith. After such a fine performance, there was real
disappointment when Mangnall's men failed to score in consecutive
away matches, losing 1-0 at Bradford City and Blackburn Rovers. At
Bradford, a United side missing the injured Meredith and Bell were
beaten by a Peter Logan goal. They were unlucky to come up against
an inspired performance from home 'keeper Mark Mellors, who was
to play an important part in the forthcoming FA Cup competition.

John Sheldon had replaced Meredith for his debut and by the time he
was to leave Old Trafford in November 1913 the wingman had made
just twenty-six first-team appearances before he joined Liverpool.
Sheldon was almost certainly the ring-leader for the betting scandal
surrounding the match between his new and old club in April 1915.
The lifting of his suspension following the ending of the war allowed
him to play another two seasons of post-war football at Anfield.

18

INTO **1911**

After suffering consecutive defeats, there was relief when, on 2 January 1911, there was a 1-0 success at home to Bradford City. Four days later, United ended their losing sequence against Nottingham Forest when goals from Homer, Picken and Wall and an own goal were enough to win 4-2. Despite the match featuring six goals, it was not the best.

The period in between the two games saw the public's attention focused on the Siege of Sidney Street, an event captured by newsreel cameras. Before Christmas, a botched robbery by Latvian anarchists had seen three police officers shot dead and another two injured. A century on, it is still the single worst incident for British police in peacetime. On 2 January, the police discovered two men were hiding out at 100 Sidney Street, Stepney. However, 200 armed officers couldn't remove the men as they were well armed and had plenty of ammunition. Support was needed from a detachment of Scots Guards, but even then the Latvians appeared impregnable and their fight only ended when the house caught fire and they burned to death on 3 January 1911. The siege became a media sensation for the time, as the first films were showing in West End cinemas that same evening and they were later shown across the rest of Britain. In the aftermath, tough new rules on immigration were considered but Winston Churchill, at the time the Liberal Home Secretary, decided otherwise. The event nevertheless reinforced xenophobia and anti-Semitism as the anarchists were both Jewish immigrants from the Russian Empire.

The derby game at Hyde Road attracted a crowd of well over 40,000, and they saw a hard fought encounter that ended in a 1-1 draw. News that the gap over second-placed Villa had widened to three points was tempered by the news that the Birmingham club's game at Woolwich Arsenal had been abandoned with just 11 minutes remaining with the away side losing 2-1. A game that kicked off at 2.55 p.m. on a foggy January day during an era when there were no floodlights was always going to be a risk, and when the referee brought proceedings to a halt it was no surprise. When the game was finally replayed – on 15 March – Villa took home a point in a 1-1 draw.

The game against Everton at Old Trafford on 28 January 1911 demonstrated the fighting qualities of the Manchester United side. Two goals down at the interval, the home side could count themselves unfortunate when a number of their shots whistled narrowly wide. Scott in the Everton goal was in great form, and some of his punching was first class. Sheldon, in for the injured Meredith, was unlucky when his shot beat the 'keeper only to miss the goal by inches. Halse then headed against the upright, and as United went at it hammer and tongs, there was a massive appeal for a penalty when Robert Young hauled down Turnbull. The referee, after consulting with the linesman, declined to give it.

Attack after attack rained down on the Everton goal, and when Duckworth struck with a flying drive, the crowd was in total uproar. Playing remarkably fine football, the United side pushed the Everton defence – including, by this time, a number of the Everton forwards – further and further back before Wall scored with a shot that Scott handled but could not stop. The resulting roar was the loudest that had been heard at Old Trafford since its opening.

After beating Aston Villa 2-1 at home in a thrilling FA Cup tie before a record crowd of 65,101, United's good form continued with consecutive League victories. The first was a 3-1 defeat of 1909 Cup finalists, Bristol City. Hugh Edmonds made his debut for United after the Bolton reserve was signed to replace the injured Moger. By appearing in the final thirteen League matches of the season the 'keeper collected a championship medal.

Newcastle were then beaten 1-0 at St James' Park, with Halse scoring an opportunist goal that gave the League leaders two deserved points. However, any hopes of recapturing the FA Cup were wiped away in the following match when West Ham United, then of the Southern League, won 2-1 at the Boleyn Ground. Victory came courtesy of a big slice of fortune when Danny Shea, a brilliant ball player whose twenty-seven goals in 1913/14 helped Blackburn win Division One, miskicked to send Edmondson, playing in place of the injured Moger, the wrong way for the first goal, but overall the result was a fair one, even after Turnbull equalised when he put the ball beyond George Kitchen. The Hammers 'keeper made 205 first-team appearances in Cup and Southern League for the club, and marked his debut by scoring from the penalty spot against Swindon Town on the opening day of the 1905/06 season. Kitchen, who had been a professional golfer before he decided to concentrate on football, was to score six goals during his time at Upton Park. West Ham's winner, which caused pandemonium among a packed crowd in which every available space was occupied, was scored by speedy left-winger Tommy Caldwell.

West Ham was founded in 1895 as Thames Ironworks, which was a local shipyard and ironworks that had built the world's first all-iron warship, HMS *Warrior*, launched in 1860. On 1 February 1911, the last ever vessel produced at the works was launched. HMS *Thunderer* was the last and largest warship ever built on the River Thames, and after her completion, her builders declared bankruptcy.

In 1900, Britain had 49 battleships and Germany just 14, with France 23 and Russia 16. Germany's naval expansion meant that by 1914 they would have 40 battleships, and this led to demands in 1909 for six new 'super Dreadnoughts'. When the Treasury argued there was only finance for four, the two general elections in 1910 saw the cry of 'we want eight, and we won't wait' go up. This produced a compromise of four ships in 1910 and four the following year.

Thunderer was 22,000 tons, with ten new 13.5-inch guns in super-firing turrets. Military expenditure among the six (the four countries named above plus Italy and Austria-Hungary) great powers jumped from £205 million in 1900 to £288 million in 1910, and it was to rise to £397 million four years later. By this time, Germany's industrial might – which had surpassed Britain's a year earlier – made it possible to challenge the British Empire, already under pressure from demands for independence in occupied countries, by also utilising what was by this time the largest ever army ever assembled in peacetime – 2.2 million in 1913. This was 800,000 more than the second largest army, which was Russia's. In comparison, Britain's was just 160,000, and this was one of the reasons why many footballers were pushed into the front line during the war and were killed as a result.

West Ham were to go down 3-2 in the following round against Blackburn Rovers, who then lost heavily against Bradford City

3-0 in the semi-final. Bradford's place in the final was a remarkable achievement considering the club had only been formed in 1903.

As the 'wool capital of the world' in the nineteenth century, Bradford grew rapidly during the industrial revolution and many migrants from Ireland were attracted there following the Potato Famine of 1845–52. Although work was plentiful, it was hard and poorly paid, while the constant outpouring of black, sulphurous smoke from factory chimneys gained the city the reputation of being the most polluted in England and ensured that many of its inhabitants died at a young age.

Against firm favourites and Cup holders Newcastle United in the final at the Crystal Palace, the Yorkshire side drew 0-0 in an uninspiring match watched by 69,068.

The replay was held at Old Trafford on Wednesday 26 April 1911. It was the first time that Manchester had hosted the Cup final since 1893, when Wolves beat Everton 1-0 at Fallowfield. This was at the time the only enclosure big enough to accommodate the ever increasing numbers wanting to attend the FA Cup final. In the event, while the area of the ground was ample, there was little stand accommodation, the overall arrangements were inadequate and a complete fiasco was only narrowly averted.

Not surprisingly, the awarding of the match was seen as recognition that Old Trafford was now the best equipped ground in the country. According to the *Manchester Evening News*,

> At the Crystal Palace the shilling spectator is very badly catered for, but at Old Trafford he will find huge embankments round three parts of the field, and from any portion a full view of the game can be obtained. On these terraces there is ample room for some 45,000 people, while the stands will hold another 20,000 people.

The paper, though, was concerned that travel arrangements to and from the ground could do with improving.

Local railway companies, meanwhile, made arrangements to organise excursion trains from a variety of points with cheap tickets to be issued from a 50-mile radius of Manchester. Both sides were expected to be well supported, and some 'lively scenes' were anticipated from early morning as arrivals poured into Manchester looking to eat and drink heartily before making their way to the ground. Owners of horse-drawn vehicles and taxi-cabs were looking forward to a profitable day's trade.

Secretary-manager Ernest Mangnall had been overwhelmed by postal requests for tickets and was forced to call on his assistant Mr T. Wallwork plus W. Armstrong and C. Jones for assistance. Imagine the Manchester United manager handling ticket requests today! Owing to the time factor, it was agreed to reserve only 5s (25p) tickets – a total of just 2,000. The other prices to be charged were 2s 6d (12.5p) and 2s (10p) and 1s (5p) on the popular side. There would be no half-prices for boys – or girls.

Ernest Mangnall had also discussed policing arrangements with Superintendent Keys. Sixty turnstiles would be opened at 1.00 p.m., 150 minutes before kick-off, and there was keen anticipation of a great game in the days leading up to it.

On the day itself, around 15,000 spectators were inside the ground at 1.30 p.m. and by 2.15 p.m., these numbers had trebled. The Yorkshire side had more of their followers at the game but the Tynesiders followers were the more noticeable in their distinctive black and white colours. Both sets of fans had their fair share of clanging bells, strident trumpets and large, creaking rattles.

The holder's preparations were upset by injuries to key players Peter McWilliam and Albert Shepherd, who finished as top scorer in Division One with Bolton Wanderers in 1905/06 and with Newcastle in 1910/11.

In the event, the game was not the greatest and there was just one goal when Bradford captain Jimmy Speirs, one of eight Scots in the Bradford side, netted after 15 minutes. The Scottish international later volunteered to join the Queen's Own Cameron Highlanders in 1915. He was decorated for his bravery at the Second Battle of Arras in April 1917, and he rose to Sergeant two months later. He was killed during the Battle of Third Ypres on or about 20 August 1971, aged thirty-one. He is buried at Dochy Farm New British Cemetery, near Ypres in Belgium. Speirs' medal has been on show at the Bradford City Museum in recent times.

Having lost 2-1 earlier in the season at home to Middlesbrough, Manchester United seemed set to enact revenge when the sides met at Ayresome Park on 4 March 1911. Middlesbrough had seen their chairman, Lieutenant T. Gibson Poole, banned from the game after events prior to the big match with local rivals Sunderland on 3 December 1910. Gibson Poole was standing as the Tory candidate in the forthcoming general election, and he persuaded some of Boro's players to speak up on his behalf. Before kick-off, Boro manager

Andy Walker offered Sunderland's captain Charlie Thomson £10 for himself and £2 each for the other Sunderland players to throw the match in order 'to help the chairman win the election'. Thomson reported the events and the FA were quickly involved. Sunderland lost the game 1-0, Gibson Poole lost the election and Walker and Poole were suspended permanently. The off-the-field scandal was to badly effect on-field events, as Boro took just nine points from the twenty-two games that followed.

Two first-half goals at Ayresome Park from West and Wall appeared to have given the away side an impregnable lead against a side struggling for form and there was therefore relief among home fans when Tom Dixon and then Bob Gibson scored after the interval. Thanks to three good Edmondson saves from Pentland, Call and Dixon, the away side left with a point. With Villa losing 1-0 at Sheffield Wednesday, the title was now moving towards Old Trafford.

Consecutive home successes followed quickly. Preston North End were walloped 5-0, with the away side falling behind very early on when Duckworth beat McBride with a fine shot. West and Connor added two more before the interval, and there were late efforts from West and Turnbull. Meredith was in great form and Hofton made an impressive home debut.

Tottenham Hotspur, in a game held over due to the FA Cup game with Villa, were beaten 3-2. The Londoners were unlucky when after being forced to play into a strong wind in the first half, they swapped ends only to find the wind had completely changed direction. Meredith's magic created the opening goal for Turnbull, and the scorer then made West's goal before Meredith made it 3-0. Two late Spurs goals gave the away side some reward for a battling performance.

Three days later, however, a very poor away performance and a mistake by Donnelly, which gave away the goal, resulted in their first League defeat in 1911, with Notts County beating Manchester United 1-0 at Meadow Lane. A 0-0 draw at home to Oldham Athletic, who conceded just forty-one League goals in the thirty-eight-match season, showed the title was by no means won, especially as two days later Aston Villa won one of their two games in hand by beating Newcastle United 2-1 at Villa Park. With a game in hand, Villa were two points behind the leaders and had a slightly superior goal average. Sunderland were back in third place, six points off the top. The two top sides, meanwhile, were set to meet in the penultimate match of the season.

Two valuable points were earned in the match at home to Liverpool on April Fool's Day, when two goals from West ensured a 2-0 success. The United forward was only denied a hat-trick by a series of superb saves by Sam Hardy in a match in which Meredith was also outstanding. The following weekend, an easy 3-0 success away to relegation threatened Bury was celebrated with extra gusto when news came through that Villa has surprisingly lost 2-0 at home to Preston North End after Arthur Mounteney scored twice late in the match.

When Manchester United entered the field for the fourth last game of the season against Sheffield United at home, they led Villa by two points and had a superior goal average. This was cut to just one following a 1-1 draw on a day when Villa won 2-1 away to Notts County. An early West penalty miss combined by an impressive display in the Blades goal from Lievesley meant the championship chasers had to settle for a point. Two days later, Manchester United played out a 0-0 draw at Sheffield Wednesday, their first-ever point at Hillsborough. The side was forced to make do without Roberts and Stacey, who had joined Duckworth and Wall on the injured list. Despite the changes, the leaders played well in the first period before fading in the second on a day in which Villa did not play.

The gap between the sides was just two, and Villa had a game in hand with the next match to be at Villa Park between the pair. Victory for Villa would put them in pole position to win the title for a second year. With difficult away games to follow at Blackburn and Liverpool, Villa was desperate for victory.

As a firmly established club, Villa had long published a weekly, *The Villa News and Record,* that cost one penny in 1911. The copy for 22 April 1911, the day of the game between the top two in the League, recognised the importance of the occasion with the editor's front page note hoping that 'today, Villa make no mistake ... and there must be no half-way doings.' A victory for the away side would to all intents and purposes confirm the championship was theirs. In a reference to the past, the editor noted that while Liverpool, would have only pride to play for the following Saturday, the Merseysiders might still want revenge for the final day of the 1898/99 season when the pair had clashed with the title at stake. Villa had won 5-1 and it was felt that Tom Watson, the Liverpool manager, would not be lying down when Villa came to Anfield.

The *News and Record* published the teams in the traditional 2-3-5 line-up for the time. In the event of any change to the line-ups, a board was taken round the track around the pitch giving the details. The sides lined up as follows:

Villa: Anstey, Lyons, Miles, Tranter, Buckley, Hunter, Wallace, Gerrish, Hampton, Bache, Henshall.

United: Edmunds, Hofton, Stacey, Duckworth, Whalley, Bell, Meredith, Halse, West, Turnbull, Conners.

The referee was Mr T. G. Rowbotham of Nottingham.

The Villa side bore a familiar look with Chris 'Ticker' Buckley at centre-half, Joe Bache at inside-right and Harry Hampton at centre-forward.

The game attracted tremendous interest, and there was a crowd of 51,000 inside Villa Park, including many who had travelled from Manchester for the occasion. Hampton's irresistible dash put the away side on the back foot almost from the start, and it was a surprise that it took until the 20th minute before the home side opened the scoring when Charlie Wallace took advantage of a Whalley foul to float a free-kick into the box where it was met powerfully by a Bache header. It took Manchester United just 5 minutes to equalise when a long ball was seized upon by Halse, who from 20 yards swerved a shot away from Brendel Anstey and into the net off the post.

Bache was a player who, with the ball at his feet, was difficult to dislodge, and his darting run took him past Duckworth and Hofton and from his splendid centre, Hampton headed home to make it 2-1. The crowd inside Villa Park roared its delight and the score remained the same at the interval. With the wind behind them, it was thought that Manchester United would be able to exert some pressure on their opponents' defence, but Wallace increased the Villa advantage when after working his way out wide, his centre was just the right height for Horace Henshall to meet and shoot home. The game was over as a contest soon after when Hofton fouled Hampton and from the resulting penalty Wallace made no mistake.

Although the game had, up to this point, been played in a good spirit, the referee soon afterwards sent off George Hunter and West after they clashed. Depending upon whether you supported Villa or United, it appears from the match reports to have decided who the aggressor was. Resulting from the incident, Mr Rowbotham awarded the away side a penalty, which Halse converted with Anstey making no attempt to save. Villa had been the better side and had deservedly taken both points to go top of the League on goal average. West's dismissal was to lead to him being suspended for the first four games of the following season, but it failed to prevent him being able to play in the final match of the 1910/11 season.

Four years later, West was suspended for much longer – until 1945 – when he was among the Liverpool and Manchester United players found guilty of 'squaring' the Easter 1915 game that resulted in two precious points for United, keeping them out of the relegation zone at the end of the season.

West headed the United scoring charts in 1910/11, 1911/12 and 1912/13. As a youngster, he was brought up by his grandparents and was a stubborn, single-minded individual who first became a coal miner. He was signed by United from Forest for a reported fee of £450, West having refused at the end of the 1909/10 season to re-sign for Forest at the terms offered to him. He was due a benefit match in 1910/11 with the Nottingham side and under recently introduced rules, he may well have received a considerable share of the transfer fee. West was also a good cricketer and played for Lancashire County Cricket's second XI.

In the match with Liverpool at Old Trafford in April 1915, West was reported – especially in the second half – to have regularly kicked the ball out of play in a game in which the bookmakers were relieved of a considerable sum when it ended in a 2-0 victory for the home side.

West learned of his suspension just before Christmas 1915. The most remarkable fact was that he was the only one of the three United players suspended who had actually played in the match. West was the only one of those suspended who refused to admit he was guilty, and he went to his deathbed protesting his innocence. When the other players had their suspensions overturned – on grounds they had played their part in the war effort by either signing up or working a reserved occupation and also admitted their part in fixing the result of the 1915 game – West's refusal to do the latter counted against him and he remained locked out of football, even being banned from entering Old Trafford to watch a match.

His attempts to organise a defence campaign ultimately came to nothing, and his suspension was only lifted as part of the celebrations that followed the successful conclusion to the Second World War.

In 2003, Graham Sharpe, wrote *Free the Manchester United One: The Inside Story of Football's Greatest Scam*. My view is that Sharpe's conclusion is correct when he writes: 'I have established that there is little or no genuine evidence which can be interpreted as conclusive proof of the guilt of Enoch West as charged.'

FINAL DAY SUCCESS

Two days after beating Manchester United in April 1911, Aston Villa travelled to Ewood Park to face Blackburn Rovers. The away side were accompanied by a small band of supporters, and also in the grandstand were a number of Manchester United players no doubt hoping to see a home victory. The key moment of the game came when Wallace missed a penalty kick, a feat he was to repeat two seasons later in the FA Cup final against Sunderland. The Ewood Park miss caused jubilation among the Manchester United players as it meant their chances of winning the title were still alive.

The goalless draw with Blackburn pushed Villa a point ahead of their nearest rivals, and they would win the title if they won or drew at Anfield and Manchester United failed to win by three clear goals. In the event that Villa drew 1-1 at Liverpool and Manchester United won 2-0, then the two sides would have tied for the title and a deciding match would be required to decide who collected the League trophy.

Prior to the last match – both sides had played 37 games. Villa 51 points with a goal average of 1.79. Manchester United 50 points with a goal average of 1.72.

The United programme for the game with Sunderland on 29 April 1911 expressed a confidence that the League trophy was coming to Old Trafford for the first time, commenting:

Nobody belittles the task of conquering Sunderland, but the odds on the United doing so are a shade better than those on Aston Villa getting the better of Liverpool at Anfield Road ... but whether or not the Championship flag flies at Old Trafford next September, the United team have merited the heartiest recommendation for the splendid exhibitions they have furnished this season ... apart from the splendid League programme, the Cup-Tie with Aston Villa, and the replayed FA Cup final would alone make any season memorable. The excellence of the team combined with the splendid accommodation provided for spectators attracted the largest gates in the League, and, despite the lavish expenditure, the club will finish the season with a substantial balance in hand on the season's working.

Sunderland had entertained their own championship hopes for much of the 1910/11 season. The Roker Park club had last finished top in 1901/02, but in October 1904 an FA investigation found Sunderland guilty of making illegal payments to players. Directors and manager Alex Mackie were suspended. Mackie was replaced by Robert Kyle in 1905, and he was to remain until 1928. A third place finish in 1908/09 was certain to be repeated in 1910/11, and under Kyle the north-east club were to win the title in 1912/13. In March 1911, Charlie Buchan was signed and after a poor start, in which he had to be persuaded to stay by trainer Billy Williams, the Londoner became one of England's finest-ever forwards and remains Sunderland's record League scorer with 209 goals.

Buchan lined up for Sunderland in front of a small, pessimistic crowd for the final game of the season at Old Trafford. Incessant rain made both watching and playing conditions difficult. The away side started the match brightly, and Jackie Mordue and Low both had shots charged down. Two half-chances were then wasted before West and Turnbull snatched at the ball when well placed. West then bundled home on 12 minutes, but to the disappointment of the United faithful the goal was disallowed due to the ball having crossed the dead ball line before Duckworth centred it. There was then further disappointment when Mordue eluded Stacey and his centre travelled neatly to George Holley, who beat Edmondson to put his side 1-0 ahead.

It took only 3 minutes for the home side to fashion an equaliser when Turnbull headed home after Tom Tait and Harry Forster hesitated when the ball bounced around in front of the Sunderland goal.

With 5 minutes of the first half remaining, the small crowd was dancing around the large terraces when West, craning every muscle, got his head onto a well-placed Meredith corner and the ball rushed past Bill Worrall. Five minutes later, it was 3-1 when Halse netted. When the referee's whistle sounded for the end of the half, every eye in the house turned towards the half-time scoreboard, which had been introduced at the start of the season to coincide with the launch of the programme. The game was listed at A – eight games stretching down to H were listed at each home game.

News that Aston Villa were losing 2-1 naturally caused great jubilation among home fans and players. With the wind in their favour, there was never any doubt that winning side would maintain the momentum during the second half, and Worrall was forced to make a series of early saves to keep his side in the game.

When, from a Meredith centre, Halse made it 4-1, the game was won and if it had not been for some fine defensive play by Milton and Forster, the home side would have been well out of sight. An under pressure Milton put through his own net to make it 5-1, after which the game remained locked in the away half with Worrall saving frequently. When the referee sounded the whistle, a famous victory by five goals to one had been achieved. The result taking Manchester United's goal average up to 1.8, meaning a draw for Aston Villa would not be good enough to win the title.

In the event, Aston Villa were beaten 3-1 at Anfield. Villa had been taken for special training at Southport following the match with Blackburn Rovers and were at full-strength.

The away side were cheered on to the pitch by a large, extremely noisy travelling support, who hoped to see their side retain the title they had captured twelve months earlier. The match was played at a sensational pace in the first 25 minutes as each side attacked at will before Ron Orr belted home a loose ball to give Anstey no chance. Soon after, the Liverpool 'Little Man' made it 2-0 and although Walters reduced the arrears, the away side left the field a goal behind at the break. The champions would have heard that their nearest rivals were winning comfortably and may well have worked out they would need to win in order to hang onto the championship trophy.

The second half was a scrappy affair, and Hampton was guilty of a poor foul when Hardy was unable to grab the ball. Villa were making some pretty movements, but the Liverpool 'keeper was rarely busy and for much of the half, the game was conducted in the middle of the park, with each side committing a large number of fouls. A desperate charge forward by the away side in the final

10 minutes largely failed to stir the Liverpool rearguard before the game – and Villa's title chances – were ended in the final minute when John McDonald neatly finished off a Harry Uren cross. The final score was Liverpool 3 Aston Villa 1 and, as a result, the League champions – for the second time in four seasons – was Manchester United. Two League titles, an FA Cup and one Charity Shield was now the record, with a second tilt at the Charity Shield to come.

The title success in 1910/11 was, if anything, a greater feat than the one of 1907/08. In the first success, Manchester United had been fortunate in largely avoiding injuries to their players until after the title was as good as won and seven players made more than thirty (from thirty-eight) League appearances with four other players also making more than twenty-five. In 1910-11, five players made more than 30 appearances and just two made more than twenty-five. The end of the season saw Ernest Mangnall constantly having to change his side due to injuries, and the signing of Hugh Edmonds as Moger's replacement was a big gamble that paid off.

Between January and April 1911, the champions were defeated just twice – at Notts County and Aston Villa – in the League.

Top of the Table

Man United	52
Aston Villa	51
Sunderland	45
Everton	45
Bradford City	45

Second Charity Shield Success

25 September 1911 (1911 Charity Shield)
Manchester United 8 (Halse 6, Turnbull, Wall), Swindon Town 4 (Fleming, Wheatcroft, Tout, Jefferson)
Man Utd: Edmonds, Hofton, Stacey, Duckworth, Roberts, Bell, Meredith, Hamil, Halse, Turnbull, Wall.
Swindon Town: Skiller, Kay, Trout, Handley, Bannister, Silto, Jefferson, Fleming, Wheatcroft, Bown, Lamb.

Manchester United faced Southern League champions Swindon Town in the 1911 Charity Shield at Stamford Bridge on

25 September 1911. This was the fourth time that the Football League champions had faced their Southern League counterparts and since United had defeated QPR in 1908, each league had won once. In 1909 Newcastle United beat Northampton Town 2-0, but in 1910 Brighton and Hove Albion beat Aston Villa 1-0. The final match between the two leagues was to come in 1912, when Blackburn Rovers beat QPR 2-1 but, as the Football League asserted its authority, the decision was taken after the war to drop the Southern League in favour of allowing the Division One champions to face the FA Cup winners.

The key player for Swindon was Harold Fleming, whose eleven appearances for England makes him the only Robins player to have represented his country. He scored nine times in these games; including a hat-trick against Ireland in Dublin on 10 February 1912. During the First World War, Fleming worked as a physical education instructor. A road has been named after him close to Swindon's County Ground, and there is a statue to him in the club's foyer. Fleming was to score the opening goal against Manchester United, but it was to be the League champions who took home the trophy in a thrilling game that was played in a sporting manner.

Taking advantage of Robert's absence for treatment following an early injury, Fleming headed home a fine Archie Bown cross on 6 minutes. Within 2 minutes, Halse created the space to find Turnbull to make it 1-1. Soon after, Halse showed good pace to pull away from the Swindon defenders before easily beating Len Skiller. The lead was maintained when Edmonds dived full length to push the ball away from the feet of the on-rushing Bown, and then following indecision in the Swindon box after a corner, Halse doubled the United advantage.

A run by Fleming then found Bob Jefferson, and from his centre Freddy Wheatcroft headed home to reduce the arrears only for Halse to again double them just 2 minutes later. With 43 minutes on the clock, the Southern side were back in the match when following the award for a penalty after Hofton tackled Wheatcroft, full-back Billy Tout scored.

The second half started at a more leisurely pace than the first, and for the first quarter of an hour both sides seemed to be taking a breather before Halse netted after his feint sent the Swindon rearguard off-balance on 63 minutes. After notching his fifth goal, the United forward repeated his feint and netted his sixth of the match to take the score to 7-3.

Swindon may have been beaten, but after Wall made it 8-3, Jefferson scored with the final kick of the match, at the conclusion of which Sir Charles Wakefield presented the Charity Shield and medals to Manchester United.

The victory brought to an end the era of the first great Manchester United side in which five trophies – two League titles, one FA Cup and two Charity Shields – were won. It was to be well over thirty years – and two world wars – before Matt Busby revived the Old Trafford club and paved the way for further successes.

The side that captured the Charity Shield in 1911/12, struggled during the season itself and finished in thirteenth place. A fourth place finish in 1912/13 was followed by a fourteenth place finish in 1913/14, and by the time United finished in eighteenth place in 1914/15, Mangnall had departed to manage Manchester City. Considering the damage he had done to the Citizens by signing many of their stars in late 1906, perhaps he felt he owed them a favour?

Manchester United's Record in 1910/11
All home games were at Old Trafford

September
Arsenal [A] 2-1
Blackburn Rovers [H] 3-2
Nottingham Forest [A] 1-2
Manchester City [H] 2-1
Everton [A] 1-0

October
Sheffield Wednesday [H] 3-2
Bristol City [A] 1-0
Newcastle United [A] 1-0
Tottenham Hotspur [A] 2-2
Middlesbrough [H] 1-2

November
Preston North End [A] 2-0
Notts County [H] 0-0
Oldham Athletic [A] 3-1
Liverpool [A] 2-3

December
Bury [H] 3-2
Sheffield United [A] 0-2
Aston Villa [H] 2-0
Sunderland [A] 2-1
Arsenal [H] 5-0
Bradford City [A] 0-1
Blackburn Rovers [A] 0-1

January
Bradford City [H] 1-0
Nottingham Forest [H] 4-2
Blackpool [A] FA Cup 2-1
Manchester City [A] 1-1
Everton [H] 2-2

February
Aston Villa [H] FA Cup 2-1
Bristol City [H] 3-1
Newcastle United [A] 1-0
West Ham United [A] FA Cup 1-2

March
Middlesbrough [A] 2-2
Preston North End [H] 5-0
Tottenham Hotspur [H] 3-2
Notts County [A] 0-1
Oldham Athletic [H] 0-0

April
Liverpool [H] 2-0
Bury [A] 3-0
Sheffield United [H] 1-1
Sheffield Wednesday [A] 0-0
Aston Villa [A] 2-4
Sunderland [H] 5-1

Final League Table

	Points
Manchester United	52

(Home: 14-4-1, 47-18; Away: 8-4-7, 25-22)

Aston Villa	51

(Home: 5-3-1 50-18; Away: 7-4-8, 19-23)

Sunderland	45
Everton	45
Bradford City	45

Appearances

	League	FA Cup
Stacey	36	3
Meredith	35	3
Turnbull	35	3
West	35	3
Roberts	33	3
Bell	27	3
Wall	26	3
Moger	25	2
Duckworth	22	3
Halse	23	2
Donnelly	15	3
Picken	14	1
Whalley	15	-
Edmonds	13	1
Livingstone	10	-
Hofton	9	-
Holden	8	-
Connor	7	-
Homer	7	-
Linkson	7	-
Curry	5	-
Sheldon	5	-
Hodge	2	-
Hooper	2	-
Blott	1	-
Hayes	1	-

Scorers

	League	FA Cup
West	19	1
Turnbull	18	1
Halse	9	1
Homer	6	-
Wall	5	1
Meredith	5	-
Picken	4	1
Duckworth	2	-
Connor	1	-
Roberts	1	-
Own goals	2	-

The following were signed to play in the 1910/11 season:

Enoch West was top scorer in Division One in 1907/08 when he notched twenty-eight goals for Nottingham Forest. West also scored three times for Forest in a 6-1 thrashing for Ernest Mangnall's side in the 1909/10 season, at the end of which he was signed to replace Jimmy Turnbull and lead Manchester United's attack. He did well and was to finish as top scorer, with nineteen League goals in 1910/11, helping his new club to a second title success in four seasons. He also top-scored in the 1911/12 and 1912/13 seasons, but his form was on the slide when League football was suspended at the end of the 1914/15 season, after which West was one of those suspended for his alleged – he always maintained his innocence – part in the fixing of the Manchester United–Liverpool relegation battle in April 1915.

John Sheldon: One of a handful of players to represent both Manchester United and Liverpool, he attempted to utilise his inside knowledge of both clubs by playing the key role in fixing the April 1915 match between the sides that Manchester United won 2-0, a result that cost bookmakers a pretty packet and led to Sheldon and three other Liverpool and Manchester United players being suspended from football. These were later lifted and Sheldon added to his twenty-six games with Manchester United a further 147 with Liverpool.

Leslie Hofton cost United £1,000 when he signed from Glossop in July 1910. The move attracted criticism in the press because he required a knee operation, and it was only after he recovered quickly that the complaint by Glossop about not being paid the agreed fee was resolved. Sadly, another injury, this time while he was playing for the Football League, prematurely ended his career and he made just eighteen first team appearances for Manchester United.

Tom Homer joined Manchester United, along with Arthur Hooper from Kidderminster Harriers, in October 1909, and four months later he scored Manchester United's second in the first game at Old Trafford. This was one of eight goals in seventeen League appearances during the 1909/10 season, and he also proved a more than able replacement when Enoch West was absent during the 1910/11 season, with Homer scoring six goals in only seven League appearances. In the circumstances, he was unfortunate not to have played sufficient matches to qualify for a League winners' medal. A knee injury the following season brought his promising time at Old Trafford to a premature end.

BIBLIOGRAPHY

Behind the Glory: 100 Years of the PFA, John Harding; *50 Years of Football 1884–1934*, Sir Frederick Wall (Class Reprint – Soccer Books Ltd 2006); *The Story of Association Football*, J. A. H. Catton [Tityrus] (Classic Reprint – Soccer Books 2006); *Purnell's Encyclopedia of Association Football* (1972); *The Hamlyn Book Of World Soccer*, Peter Arnold & Christopher David (1973); *Those Feet: A Sensual History of English Football*, David Winner; *League Football and the Men Who Made It: The Official Centenary History of the Football League*, Simon Inglis (1988); *The People's Game: The History Of Football Revisited*, James Walvin; *Through The Turnstiles*, Brian Tabner; *Golden Boot: Football's Top Scorers*, Mark Metcalf & Tony Matthews; *Who's Who Of Arsenal, Aston Villa, Everton, Liverpool, Stoke City, Wolverhampton Wanderers*, Tony Matthews; *Barnsley*, Granville Firth & David Wood; *Derby County*, Gerald Mortimer; *Newcastle United*, Paul Joannou; *Manchester United, Notts County, Oldham Athletic*, Garth Dykes; *Preston North End*, Dean Hayes; *Sunderland*, Garth Dykes & Doug Lamming; *Spurs Alphabet*, Bob Goodwin; *Birmingham City: The Complete Record*, Tony Matthews; *Blackburn Rovers: The Complete Record*, Mike Jackson; *Blackpool: The Complete Record*, Roy Calley; *Manchester City: The Complete Record*, Gary James; *Middlesbrough: The Complete Record*, Harry Glasper; *Sunderland: The Complete Record*, Mike Gibson, Rob Mason & Barry Jackson; *The FA Cup*, Mike Collett; *West Ham United*, Tony Hogg;

The Clarets Chronicles: The Definitive History of Burnley Football Club 1888–2007, Ray Simpson; *Bolton Wanderers FC: The Official History 1877–2002*, Simon Marland; *Everton FC: The Men from the Hill Country*, Tony Onslow; *History Of Blackburn Rovers 1875–1925*, Charles Francis (Class Reprint – Soccer Books Ltd 2005); *Football Wizard: The Billy Meredith Story*, John Harding; *All Shook Up: Bury's Amazing Cup Story 1900 & 1903*, Mark Metcalf; *Free The Manchester United One*, Graham Sharpe; *Origins Of The Football League: The First Season 1888/89*, Mark Metcalf; *Red Dawn – Manchester United in the Beginning: From Newton Heath to League Champions*, Brian Belton; *Old Trafford: 100 Years at the Theatre of Dreams*, Iain McCartney; *The Forgotten Legends*, Charbel Boujaoude, Iain McCartney & Frank Colbert; *In Search of the Double: Sunderland AFC 1912/13*, Paul Days & Mark Metcalf; *Sheffield United: Champions 1897/98*, Nick Udall; *Bright Red: The Liverpoo–Manchester United Matches*, Mark Metcalf, Tony Bugby & Leslie Millman; *Lifting The Cup: The Story of Battling Barnsley 1910–12*, Mark Metcalf & David Wood; *Manchester – The City Years*, Gary James; *Manchester United's Golden Age 1903–1914*, Thomas Taw; *The Making of the English Working Class*, E. P. Thompson; *The Age Of Empire: 1875–1914*, Eric Hobsbawm; *Culture in Manchester: Institutions and Urban Change Since 1850*; *Who Owns Britain*, Kevin Cahill; *Durham Miners Millennium Book*, Dave Temple; *Yesterday's Britain*, Reader's Digest; *The Ragged Trousered Philanthropist*, Robert Tressell; *Liberty's Dawn: A People's History of the Industrial Revolution*, Emma Griffin; *Engels*, John Green; *The Workers' Union*, Richard Hyman.